BLIMPS AND U-BOATS

BLIMPS

Naval Institute Press
Annapolis, Maryland

& U-BOATS

J. Gordon Vaeth

U.S. Navy Airships in the Battle of the Atlantic

Library of Congress Cataloging-in-Publication Data

Vaeth, J. Gordon (Joseph Gordon), 1921–
    Blimps and U-boats : U.S. Navy airships in the battle of the
Atlantic / J. Gordon Vaeth.
        p.   cm.
    Includes bibliographical references and index.
    ISBN 1-55750-876-3
    1. World War, 1939–1945—Aerial operations, American.
2. Airships—History.   3. Antisubmarine warfare—History.   4. World
War, 1939–1945—Naval operations, German.   5. World War,
1939–1945—Naval operations—Submarine.   6. United States.
Navy—Aviation—History.   I. Title.
D790.V34   1992
940.54′4973—dc20   91-37161

Printed in the United States of America on acid-free paper ∞

9 8 7 6 5 4 3 2

First printing

*To all who saw duty with airships,
in the air and on the ground, during the Second World War.*

CONTENTS

PREFACE

WHEN IN JANUARY 1942 German submarines began their attacks on shipping in American waters, the U.S. Navy had one squadron of four blimps based at Lakehurst, New Jersey.

Before the war ended, there would be eleven antisubmarine blimp squadrons deployed along the east coasts of North and South America, throughout the Caribbean, at the Strait of Gibraltar, and in the Mediterranean.

This is an account of blimp operations as I knew them from having served as air intelligence officer to Commo. George H. Mills, Atlantic Fleet airship type commander.

BLIMPS AND U-BOATS

1. ANTECEDENTS

THE ANTISUBMARINE BLIMP was a British development. On 28 February 1915 Admiral of the Fleet Lord Fisher, First Sea Lord, ordered an airship built for use against the U-boats of Imperial Germany. Fisher, always in a hurry, wanted it flying within three weeks.

The result was *Sea Scout #1* (*SS #1*), which was assembled out of available bits and pieces and flown successfully on 18 March. It consisted of a two-seat, single-engine airplane fuselage suspended below a hydrogen-filled bag that was fitted with stabilizing fins.

About two hundred blimps of various types and sizes followed that first Sea Scout. British airshipmen claimed that they sighted forty-nine enemy submarines and sunk twenty-seven during the war, but information now available does not substantiate those claims. The assertion, also made, that no vessel under British airship escort was torpedoed is probably true.

The British coined the term "blimp," an airship that has no internal framework and keeps its hull form by the pressure of its lifting gas. In 1915 Lt. A. D. Cunningham was inspecting *Sea Scout #1* when he playfully flicked its gas bag, also known as its envelope, with his thumb. The airship replied with something that sounded like "BLIMP." At lunch in the mess at the Capel air station where this momentous event took place, everyone had great fun trying to imitate the sound the airship had made. Before long, *SS #12* and others like it started to be called blimps. There is also a story that the word is a contraction of "B-limp," a type of British nonrigid airship. There was never any such British airship class.

A postwar analysis by a commission of the French Chamber of Deputies reported that during hostilities nonrigid airships (blimps) of the French navy sighted more than sixty submarines, but the commission said nothing about how many of them were attacked or destroyed. It did say that no vessels were sunk while under airship protection.

The U.S. Navy Department, impressed by Britain's blimp program, embarked on one of its own. During July 1916 the newly established Aircraft Division of the Bureau of Construction and Repair began work on the design of a single-engine nonrigid airship reflecting the Sea Scout design. Sixteen of these, called the B-class, were built. There was no A-class, the unsuccessful *DN-1*, a one-of-a-kind blimp ordered from the Connecticut Aircraft Company in 1915, being considered as such.

The Goodyear Tire and Rubber Company, the B. F. Goodrich Company, and the Connecticut Aircraft Company built and delivered the sixteen B-ships between July 1917 and June 1918. Goodyear's

The navy's first airship, the *DN-1*, was designed to operate from a floating hangar at Pensacola. Overweight and underpowered, it made a handful of flights in 1917 before being damaged and scrapped. (U.S. Navy)

One of the four B-class airships built for the navy by the B. F. Goodrich Company. (Author's collection)

airship assembly and test site at Wingfoot Lake, Ohio, on the outskirts of Akron, became Naval Air Station Akron, a center of lighter-than-air (LTA) flight training for the navy during the war. Upon completion, the airships were assigned to naval air stations built for them at Chatham, Massachusetts; Montauk Point and Rockaway Beach, Long Island; Cape May, New Jersey; Hampton Roads, Virginia; and Pensacola and Key West, Florida. During World War I, U.S. Navy airships were piloted by an estimated 170 officers, a number of whom went overseas to fly French-supplied airships, notably at Paimboeuf, near St. Nazaire on the Bay of Biscay. On patrol in American waters, the blimps logged 13,600 hours without a fatality. There is no record that they sighted or attacked any submarines.

B-ships carried a crew of three in an airplane fuselage hanging from the envelope. Produced by three different manufacturers, they varied somewhat in dimensions and details. A typical "B" had a volume of eighty-four thousand cubic feet, was 163 feet long, and

3

could do forty-seven miles per hour tops. The range at 35 mph was about nine hundred miles.

The B-class inevitably led to the "C," which had more than twice the volume (181 thousand cubic feet), was thirty-three feet longer (196 feet), and, powered by two engines instead of one, was faster by 13 mph (60 mph). Contracts for a total of thirty "Cs" were placed with Goodyear and Goodrich, but the number was reduced to ten when the war ended. The first of these airships, the *C-1*, began flying on 22 October 1918. The *C-5*, fitted with a carburetor arrangement that worked on gasoline or hydrogen gas, attempted a transatlantic flight in May 1919, only to be blown from its moorings in Newfoundland and out to sea with no one on board. On 5 December 1921 the *C-7* became the first airship filled with nonflammable helium to fly.

The next blimps, the D-series, had a fiery beginning and end. The *D-1* burned in its shed before it could make its first flight. The navy turned the next four "Ds" over to the army. A sixth, which combined a D-class envelope with an enclosed car built for it by the Naval Aircraft Factory in Philadelphia, also caught fire, on 21 August 1921, destroying its Rockaway Beach hangar and everything inside. The volume of the "D" was 180 thousand cubic feet.

By this time Connecticut Aircraft and Goodrich had abandoned airship construction, leaving the field to Goodyear, who would continue as the navy's sole supplier of blimps for four decades. Goodyear, it so happened, had a couple of airships of its own design that it wanted to sell. The navy bought them and called them the *E-1* and *F-1*. Single-engined, they were something of a step backward, their size being roughly that of a "B." The performance they turned in was unimpressive.

Procurement of the "Cs," "Ds," *E-1*, and *F-1* had been authorized in 1918. That summer design was begun on the G-class, a kind of superblimp of four hundred thousand cubic feet that would carry, among other things, a 3-inch cannon. No airship of this type was ever built.

In 1921 Goodyear delivered the *H-1*, a tiny roly-poly of forty-three thousand cubic feet that could be towed behind a ship as a kite balloon or cast free to operate as an airship. The navy lost the *H-1* in the fire that consumed the *D-6* at Rockaway Beach.

Because the letter "I" is easily confused with the figure "1," there was no attempt to identify an I-class.

A J-class nonrigid airship, vintage 1920s, with a kite balloon above. (U.S. Navy)

The sequence of nonrigid airship designations was resumed with the *J-1*. It had a capacity of 174,800 cubic feet and a length of 168 feet when it took to the air in 1923. There was no J-2, but the *J-3* and *J-4* arrived in 1926 and 1927, respectively. They had slightly larger envelopes than the *J-1*. By the time they entered service, all navy airships were helium-inflated.

The 320-thousand-cubic-foot *K-1* flew in 1931. This ugly duckling, ungainly in appearance and with a pronounced tail droop, was the first navy blimp to mount its car flush against the underside of its hull. It had a Goodyear-supplied envelope and a navy-supplied cabin. Inside the bag were one or more chambers to hold a propanelike gaseous fuel that could substitute for gasoline for its engines. This fuel, Blau gas, because it weighed about the same as air, could be burned with minimum effect on the buoyancy of the airship. Gasoline, on the other hand, lightened the airship by the weight of every gallon burned. The *K-1* was intended, in part, to investigate

5

the desirability of using Blau gas in navy blimps. The navy never adopted the idea.

Between the mid-1920s and the mid-1930s, except for the building of the *K-1*, there was a hiatus in the navy's development of nonrigid airships. Another airship type, the much larger and higher performance, structurally framed rigid, came upon and dominated the LTA scene. With their Duralumin framework of transverse frames or rings, joined by longitudinals and covered with cotton cloth painted aluminum color with aircraft "dope," rigid airships seemingly held enormous potential for naval and commercial uses. While a fascinated world looked on in those Golden Years of Aviation, the "big ships" flew and failed, their potential never realized.

The U.S. Navy's interest in rigid airships dated back to the first World War. In that conflict the Germans operated rigids, calling them Zeppelins for their inventor, Count Ferdinand von Zeppelin, and used them for bombing England and scouting at sea. The antiaircraft defenses developed against these hydrogen-filled giants made their raids increasingly unproductive and, eventually, suicidal. Their use for naval reconnaissance, however, was another matter. Nothing else in the air could match the Zeppelin's endurance or cruising range. Their effectiveness as naval scouts, if not proven, was promising.

Acting on this promise, the U.S. Congress voted a major postwar rigid-airship program in the Naval Bill of 1919. It provided funds for a construction and operating shed for rigids and for the purchase of one such airship overseas and the construction of another in the United States.

Accordingly, a hangar was erected and a naval air station established in the pine barrens of New Jersey near the little town of Lakehurst. The site was a former army chemical-warfare center, Camp Kendrick, that had been declared surplus and was up for sale. The navy purchased it. It also made arrangements to buy the *R-38*, a rigid the British happened to have under construction, and to bring it to America. The *R-38*, however, broke in half over the Humber River in England in 1921 on its fourth flight, too soon for it even to have had a name. Meanwhile, in the brand new hangar at Lakehurst, assembly began of a modified copy of a wartime Zeppelin, a copy to be named the USS *Shenandoah*. The *Shenandoah* would also fail in flight, destroyed by severe weather over Ohio in 1925 after two years of service.

In addition, the navy possessed a German-built rigid, the USS *Los Angeles*, delivered to Lakehurst by its constructors in 1924. Although the United States had missed out on the distribution of Germany's Zeppelins as war spoils, the "L.A." had been built with the German government paying the bill.

Despite the loss of thirty American airshipmen in the *R-38* and *Shenandoah*, Rear Adm. William A. Moffett, chief of the Bureau of Aeronautics since its creation in 1921, had been able to persuade Congress to authorize two more rigids. These would be the USS *Akron* and USS *Macon*, twin airships of 6.5 million cubic feet, designed to carry, launch, and recover hook-on fighter planes. The *Akron* first flew in September 1931, the *Macon* in April 1933. The *Akron* crashed into the Atlantic in thunderstorms off the New Jersey coast the night of 3–4 April 1933. Seventy-three of the seventy-six men on board died, including Moffett. The few survivors of what

The USS *Macon*, shown recovering two of her five F9C-2 Sparrowhawk fighters, exemplified the rigid airships that eclipsed the blimp in naval aviation for over a decade. Lost off California in 1935, her wreckage was discovered near Point Sur in 1990. (National Archives, 80-G-428442)

was then the world's worst aeronautical disaster could not present a clear picture of what had happened, whether the ship had failed structurally, or whether air currents had driven it into the sea. Two years later, on 12 February 1935, the *Macon* lost its upper fin in a gust and fell into the Pacific off Point Sur, California, with the loss of two lives.

While they operated from 1923 to 1935, the navy's rigid airships overwhelmed the smaller and not-nearly-so-spectacular nonrigids. In the heyday of the big airships, blimps attracted little attention and held little appeal for naval aviators. The navy used them mainly for training officers preparing to fly the rigids; pilots were required to make twenty flights in blimps, for a minimum of twenty hours.

After the *Macon* was lost, only the blimps remained. The *Los Angeles* had been decommissioned at Lakehurst in 1932 after 331 flights and 4,181 hours in the air. The *J-4*, which had shared the *Macon's* hangar at Naval Air Station Moffett Field, California, was

The crash of the *Macon* reawakened the navy's interest in nonrigids. The navy purchased the Goodyear blimp *Defender* and called it the *G-1*. (U.S. Navy)

deflated, shipped to Lakehurst, and reerected. In late 1935 the navy purchased the advertising blimp *Defender*, flagship of Goodyear's commercial fleet. As the *G-1*, it would be used for training and experimentation and serve as an airborne jumping platform for the parachute school at Lakehurst. There the navy's aircraft inventory also included the *K-1* and the "Tin Bubble"—a small, 202-thousand-cubic-foot, egg-shaped "metalclad" also known as the *ZMC-2*—which used helium pressure, internal framing, and an outer surface of Alclad aluminum sheeting.

These, plus a few free and kite balloons, were the extent of naval LTA craft at Lakehurst in 1936, the year Germany's *Hindenburg* came calling on its first season of regularly scheduled commercial operations across the North Atlantic. The navy's airship complement had not changed when that hydrogen-buoyed Zeppelin caught fire on 6 May 1937 and fell in flames onto the air station's landing field, killing thirty-six people.

Predictions that the *Hindenburg*'s end was the end of airships failed to come to pass. While much of the press, the public, and the navy opposed spending more money and effort on "the big ships," no one seemed to question the safety, usefulness, or reliability of nonrigids. The record of Goodyear's advertising airships to date—more than two hundred thousand passengers carried without a fatality—had much to do with their acceptance. With determination and, in view of the recency of the *Hindenburg* tragedy, no-little courage and guts, the navy proceeded in August of 1937 to order two new airships: the *L-1* and *K-2*.

Both blimps were procured under the same contract with the Goodyear-Zeppelin Corporation, the *L-1*, a small trainer, costing $65,217, the *K-2*, a large patrol airship, $162,929. The *L-1* would be a copy of a Goodyear advertising blimp, the *K-2* an entirely new design. The *K-2*'s 404,000-cubic-foot volume and 246-foot length would make it the largest blimp in existence.

The Goodyear Tire and Rubber Company had formed Goodyear-Zeppelin of Akron, Ohio in the early 1920s when it acquired rights to the patents of Luftschiffbau-Zeppelin, the German constructor of Zeppelin airships. Goodyear had acquired, also, the services of thirteen of the German company's staff. They had won for their new employer the navy's contract to build the *Akron* and *Macon*. Among those who had stayed on and become U.S. citizens were

Dr. Karl Arnstein, Goodyear-Zeppelin's director of engineering, and Hermann R. Liebert, his chief designer. These were the men who were chiefly responsible for building the *L-1* and *K-2*. Another major player was Charles P. "C. P." Burgess, airship engineer in the Bureau of Aeronautics.

The *L-1* was delivered in April 1938, the *K-2* in December. The new ships were flown from Akron to Lakehurst, at that time the center of naval LTA activity in America.

The *L-1* and *K-2* joined the *J-4, K-1, G-1*, and *ZMC-2*, as well as the *TC-14*, an airship that the navy had inherited from the army the year before when that service ended its airship operations. The navy had also inherited a twin, the *TC-13*, but its envelope needed replacement, and it would not fly with navy markings until 1940.

In May 1939, four months after its arrival at Lakehurst, the *K-2* was flown into the trees. The car, the gondola that carried the crew,

The *K-2*, prototype of 133 K-class airships to follow, before a machine gun turret and electronics were added. (U.S. Navy)

was bashed in, but there were no injuries. The bag that held the helium was punctured and deflated.

By the time the *K-2* was returned to full service, Europe was at war. As the military might of Nazi Germany became increasingly evident, America hastily set about improving its own defenses. Public Law 635, passed by the 76th Congress in June 1940, called for a "10,000 plane program." It included authorization for forty-eight nonrigid airships for the navy.

This law led to another navy contract with Goodyear for two more airships of the *L-1* type and six of the *K-2*. Goodyear-Zeppelin, meanwhile, was changing its name to Goodyear Aircraft to rid itself of the stigma of its earlier German affiliation.

Because protecting sea-lanes would be the blimps' prime mission, sites to serve as their operating bases were looked for in the Boston, Norfolk, Charleston, New Orleans, Galveston, and Straits of Florida areas. (Lakehurst would cover the New York approaches.) Locations were selected at South Weymouth, Massachusetts; Elizabeth City, North Carolina; Brunswick, Georgia; Richmond, Florida; Houma, Louisiana; and Hitchcock, Texas. A complete naval air station would be built at each.

All of the new stations would have hangars nominally a thousand feet in length. Two of the hangars would be of steel construction; the others, to save war-critical materials, would be made of wood and concrete. If of steel, they were to be 960 feet long, 200 feet high, and 330 feet wide; if of wood and concrete, except for the one at Houma, Louisiana, 1,000 × 150 × 237 feet. South Weymouth and Elizabeth City were to have one hangar of each type. There would be two wooden sheds at Brunswick, three at Richmond, and one each at Houma and Hitchcock. Houma's hangar, although a thousand-footer of wood and concrete, would have a unique design. The Louisiana soil on which it sat could not support the weight of the usual doors, requiring a door arrangement that would have unfortunate consequences.

Lakehurst had more hangar space now that the *Los Angeles* and *ZMC-2* had been dismantled and scrapped. Even so, the hangar would be inadequate for the operations and activities being planned for the station. Two smallish hangars, one for training airships and one for Lakehurst's assembly and repair shops, would be built adjoining the existing structure. Two of the new large wooden

11

hangars would be erected across the field at its southwestern corner.

To provide the pilots needed for the blimps, active-duty officers were encouraged to request assignment to LTA. The naval aviation cadet program was broadened to include airship flight training. Naval reservists, who included a number of Goodyear pilots, would be called up.

In these ways did the navy's airship arm prepare to meet the submarine threat from overseas.

2. *PAUKENSCHLAG*

ADOLF HITLER CAUGHT the German navy by surprise when he declared war against the United States four days after Japan attacked Pearl Harbor. The Kriegsmarine had no forces in place to begin hostilities in U.S. waters.

Karl Dönitz, *Befehlshaber der Unterseeboote*, commander of U-boats, immediately asked his superiors for twelve Type IX boats to carry the war to America. These were large, long-range submarines, officially 740 tonners but actually displacing nearly 1,051 tons surfaced and 1,178 tons submerged. Wanting to maintain a concentration of U-boats west of Gibraltar, the Naval High Command let him have only six, which became five when one had to drop out for repairs.

So it was that between 18 and 27 December 1941 the *U-66, U-109, U-123, U-125,* and *U-130,* sortied from Lorient on the German-occupied French coast. Theirs was Operation *Paukenschlag*, the opening U-boat offensive against America. Dönitz liked giving his groups and operations dramatic names. For this one he had chosen *Paukenschlag*, literally translated as "roll on the kettle drums," because it signaled the start of something momentous.

At ten knots the two Type IXBs and three Type IXCs plowed westward through the Atlantic. In the absence of enemy aircraft, they stayed on the surface most of the way. Their assignment was to operate independently against targets of opportunity encountered between Nova Scotia and Cape Hatteras, North Carolina. For maximum surprise and effect, Dönitz wanted all five captains to begin striking on the same day: 13 January. They were not to attack before then unless they happened upon a target of ten thousand tons or greater.

Airship Patrol Squadron Twelve, consisting then of the *K-3, K-4, K-5,* and *K-6,* had been commissioned at Lakehurst on 2 January with Lt. Comdr. Raymond F. Tyler as commanding officer. "Ty," who had been flying airships since 1918, had the rugged build and face of the tall outdoorsman that he was. A thoroughly likeable sort, considerate and understanding of junior officers, he spoke slowly and in a low-pitched but loud voice, frequently punctuating the remarks of others with "Well, I'll be damned!"

On the same day the squadron had been commissioned, so had Airship Patrol Group One. Capt. George H. Mills, Lakehurst's commanding officer since January 1940, had relinquished that duty to become the group commander. For months before the United States entered the European war, Mills had been sending the station's two "TCs," and the *K-2*, and other "Ks," as they were delivered, on daily

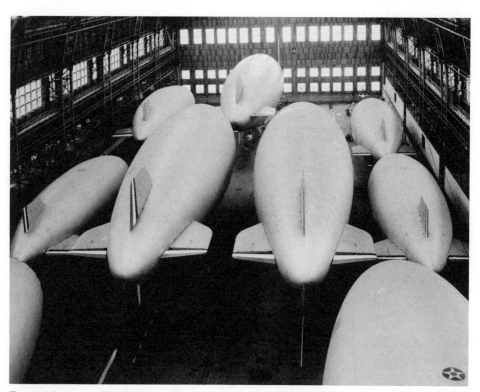

Four of Squadron Twelve's airships (the *K-3*, *K-4*, *K-5*, and *K-6*) and five of the station's airships (the *K-2*, *L-1*, *L-2*, *L-3*, and *G-1*) crowd Lakehurst's Hangar #1 in the opening days of the war. (U.S. Navy)

patrols. "Shorty" Mills had also been working to develop airship antisubmarine tactics, of which, when he took over, there were none, and he had introduced the capabilities of the K-ship, as blimps of the *K-2* class were being called, to the operating forces. Now he would be responsible for all the operational squadrons to be established along the coast. Reasonable and cooperative, this likeable, low-key officer from North Carolina had just the right personality to work well with other surface or air commanders.

Paukenschlag began earlier than Dönitz had planned. On 11 January 1942 Kapitänleutnant (Lt. Comdr.) Reinhard Hardegen, in the *U-123*, a Type IXB, found what looked like a ten thousand tonner in his sights. Launching two "eels," as the Germans called their torpedoes, he sank the 9,076-ton British steamer *Cyclops* three hundred miles east of Cape Cod.

On the official starting date, the thirteenth, Ernst Kals, commanding the *U-130*, sank two ships between Newfoundland and Nova Scotia.

Hardegen, meanwhile, was steering toward New York. On the night of the fourteenth he sent the 9,500-ton tanker *Norness* to the bottom southeast of Montauk Point, Long Island, not far from the Nantucket Lightship.

The next morning, the *K-3* of Airship Patrol Squadron Twelve was patrolling the area. The crew was unaware that the *Norness* had been sunk. An airplane approached the blimp and circled it several times, then took off headed south. The blimp's commander, Lt. (jg) Larry P. Furculow, a Goodyear pilot who had been called up, followed until he saw directly ahead what looked to be a sailboat. Actually, it was a ship's bow floating on the water; the remainder of the vessel that was attached to it rested on the bottom.

Furculow started searching for survivors. He did not know that most of them had already been picked up. Four miles away he found a raft with four men. Dropping low and heading into the wind, he throttled back and hovered overhead. His copilot, Lt. Cecil A. Bolam, reputed to be able to shout louder than almost anyone in the navy LTA community, lowered his window, leaned out, and tried to talk to the survivors. He could make out the words "Norness" and "submarine." The *K-3* advised Lakehurst and stood by, lowering water and food to the survivors until surface craft arrived to pick them up.

15

Furculow and Bolam looked for more survivors but found only an overturned lifeboat.

Now alerted to the enemy's presence, blimp crews were eager to strike back.

On 16 January an airship of Squadron Twelve depth bombed "a surfaced submarine in the process of diving."

On 18 January there was a repeat of the same.

On 22 January a blimp investigating an oil slick reported bombing two submarines that the pilot said surfaced and immediately dove right underneath it. Its radioed report brought two more K-ships to the scene. Altogether the three blimps dropped a total of nine bombs.

On 30 January three more blimps attacked an oil slick.

And on 10 February there was another attack on another oil slick.

None of these actions, all carried out in daylight, produced any

Loading a depth bomb onto a K-ship's outboard rack. (U.S. Navy)

evidence that a submarine had been destroyed, damaged, or even present. The airship crews involved were confident of what they had seen and reported, but there was not then or later any information to confirm that their targets had been German submarines or, as they thought in one case, Italian. The *Paukenschlag* boats were for the most part outside the range of Lakehurst's blimps. Only Hardegen (*U-123*) and Kals (*U-130*) had been where airships could have intercepted them.

Toward the end of January and at the beginning of February the *Paukenschlag* boats, their torpedoes expended, headed home. They had sunk twenty-five ships, for more than 150 thousand tons. High scorer had been Hardegen with nine vessels, second highest Kals with six. The five U-boat commanders would have returned with an even greater number of ships sunk had their torpedoes been more reliable. With their return, *Paukenschlag* was ended.

In January Dönitz sent five more Type IXs into U.S. waters. First was the *U-106*, the sixth of the original *Paukenschlag* group that had been forced by engine trouble to drop out. It arrived off Florida before the end of the month. The remaining four were on station farther up the coast by late in the first week of February.

In addition to the IXs, Dönitz also began sending in the smaller, medium-size Type VIICs, official tonnage 517, actual surfaced and submerged displacement 761 and 865 tons, respectively. Dönitz had dispatched a group of these boats to operate in the Newfoundland–Nova Scotia region concurrently with the *Paukenschlag* wave. Their performance had been a surprise.

The VIIC, of which more than 560 would be built, had been thought too short-ranged to make the transatlantic round-trip and still have enough diesel fuel remaining to carry out useful patrols. It turned out that by practicing fuel economies and loading the boats as never before—including putting fuel in tanks previously reserved for drinking water—the VIICs could reach America and operate offshore there for as long as two or three weeks. The VIICs would become the mainstay of Germany's underseas fleet.

For German U-boats of whatever type, American coastal shipping offered a bonanza during the first months of 1942. Vessels sailed independently, without escort, and often with running lights burning. The glare from the coast, illuminated as if there were no war, revealed the silhouettes of ships to the enemy lying in wait.

The radio transmissions of shipping were open and uncontrolled; destinations, schedules, and routing could be learned by listening in. Patrol craft, sea or air, were rare and, when encountered, showed that the Americans had yet to learn the importance of persistence in developing U-boat contacts. Dönitz's submersible torpedo boats, after lying on the bottom by day, would surface to attack by night. When they did, they picked off ship after ship, as in a shooting gallery. For Germany's submarines a second "Happy Time" was at hand, like the first off Britain early in the war.

In January 1942 the four blimps of Airship Patrol Squadron Twelve flew 705 hours; in February, when icing and severe winter winds kept them hangar-bound for eight days, 532 hours; in March, 687 hours; and in April, 1,172 hours. Meanwhile, in February and March, the Germans sank a quarter of a million tons of shipping along the coast from Maine to northern Florida, the area called the Eastern Sea Frontier, leaving coastal beaches littered with wreckage, bodies, and oil. To make matters worse, U-boats began penetrating the Caribbean in late February.

A major reason for the German successes, in addition to the American lack of ships, aircraft, and experience, was the absence of coastal convoys. These were not instituted until May. When convoys were formed, the number of merchant ship sinkings by U-boats dropped dramatically. The mix of missions flown by Squadron Twelve, which was augmented by the arrival of the *K-7* on 30 April, showed the change in emphasis from patrol to escort:

	Jan	*Feb*	*Mar*	*Apr*	*May*
Escort Flights	6	9	17	25	93
Patrol Flights	45	30	36	35	12

Blimps made three depth-bombing attacks in February, nine attacks in March, and three more in April, a month in which a pilot again reported seeing a surfaced submarine dive and disappear before he could reach the swirl it left behind and drop his bombs.

Owing to the intensity of the U-boat campaign, airships found a number of survivors of torpedoings, mostly in lifeboats in the open sea. On 11 April the *K-4* found one with survivors of a sinking that

En route to a patrol area. (U.S. Navy)

One of seventy thousand ships escorted in the Atlantic. (U.S. Navy)

had taken place two weeks before. Six days later the *K-5* sighted another lifeboat with twenty-seven people in it.

The *K-5* had begun that particular flight from the Coast Guard Air Station Elizabeth City, North Carolina, from which it was operating while awaiting the completion of the naval air station (LTA) being built down the road at Weeksville. On its first flight from the Coast Guard base on 14 April, the crew of the *K-5* had watched the destroyer *Roper* pick up bodies from a U-boat it had just destroyed. This was the *U-85*, a Type VII, the first German submarine sunk in American coastal waters.

The *K-8* was delivered on 18 May, increasing the number of airships operating in the Atlantic to six.

The claim, dating to World War I, that no surface vessel under airship escort had ever been successfully attacked by submarine fell on 25 May 1942, four miles east of Barnegat Light, New Jersey, when the *U-593* torpedoed the tanker *Persephone*.

A single airship, the *K-4*, with Lt. Charles H. Becker as pilot, was covering a convoy of twenty ships that were spread out over ten to fifteen miles of their route. From an altitude of 250 feet, Becker kept them under observation, slowly proceeding from one end of the line to the other about four thousand to six thousand yards on the seaward side. At 1510, while moving south from the van of the convoy, Becker and crew saw a billow of smoke from the sixth ship, which was about three to four miles distant. At full throttle the *K-4* went to the stricken vessel's aid. After looking unsuccessfully for some sign of a submarine, it stood by the *Persephone* while its crew, who had taken to the boats, was rescued by surface craft.

On 1 June a new lighter-than-air squadron, Airship Patrol Squadron Fourteen, was commissioned at the new Naval Air Station Elizabeth City, North Carolina, under the command of Comdr. Daniel J. Weintraub.

The next day Airship Patrol Squadron Eleven was placed in commission at the new Naval Air Station South Weymouth, Massachusetts. Lt. Comdr. Samuel M. Bailey, rather "laid back," not very talkative, yet competent, assumed command. He was overshadowed by his dynamo of an executive officer, Lt. Comdr. John J. "Fighting John" McCormick, a former submariner. "Fighting John" was loud-talking and fast-acting. He seemed to specialize, even if he didn't intend to, in scaring the wits out of junior officers, the author in-

The tanker *Persephone*, believed the only vessel torpedoed while under airship protection in two world wars, on 25 May 1942. (U.S. Navy)

cluded. But the better you got to know McCormick, the more you appreciated him.

At 0650 on 9 June the patrolling *K-3*, on loan to Squadron Eleven from Squadron Twelve, sighted a large convoy coming up over the horizon. Watching it through binoculars, the pilot suddenly saw a column of water rise from the bow of the last ship, followed quickly by a second explosion. The vessel was the freighter *Kronprinsen*, which had come within torpedo range of the *U-432*.

The *K-3* made for the scene, reaching it as the vessel's crew began to abandon ship. The blimp could find no trace of a submarine. Neither could the British destroyer and two corvettes that moved in to make a sound search. Meanwhile, the *Kronprinsen* had stopped sinking. The first explosion had holed it, so it was down by the bow. The second had practically blown the stern away. Yet it stayed

21

afloat. From what he could see, the *K-3*'s pilot believed the wreck salvageable. He so advised the escort commander, who instructed him to round up the crew members in the boats and direct them by blinker to return on board. The *K-3* did this, also radioing for tug support, which, when it arrived, took the damaged vessel in tow for Nova Scotia. The airship stayed with the freighter for more than fifteen hours. On its way back to South Weymouth, it bucked fifty-knot headwinds. When it landed, fewer than thirty gallons of fuel remained in its tanks.

In June one of the "Ks" was dunked while flying low in poor visibility. An aviation cadet was on the elevators. (After three months of ground school and 250 hours in training airships of the *L-1* variety, "avcads" at that time would spend a month flying with an operational squadron before being designated as qualified in airships.) Losing control, he let the ship descend to within a few feet of the water. Two depth bombs were jettisoned and full up elevator and throttle applied. The blimp skimmed the surface, the after part of its car going under and six feet of the lower fin as well. Then the ship climbed and continued its mission with no serious damage but a good deal of trauma on board.

It was also in June that the *K-7* gave one of the first demonstrations of what other services an airship could provide to convoys, besides the obvious one of keeping submarines away. Requested by a convoy's escort commander to contact one of his brood and tell it to take up proper position, Lt. Marion H. Eppes, unable to establish blinker communication with the vessel, decided upon a message drop. He wrote the escort commander's order on a sheet of paper, secured it at the end of a length of twine, and weighted it with a roll of friction tape. Then he made a low slow pass over the ship, streaming the line and landing the message on the bridge, whereupon the vessel took up its correct station.

Blimps of Airship Patrol Group One delivered eight attacks with negative results during June.

In July two more airships were added to the group, an increase offset by the deflation of the *K-6* at South Weymouth on the sixth. Eighty-knot winds tore the ship from the mobile mast, to which it was moored by its bow, carried it to the edge of the field, and deposited it in the trees. There were no serious injuries.

On 10 July, for the first time, a blimp provided convoy coverage

K-ship with convoy. (U.S. Navy)

all through the night. The *K-4* of Squadron Eleven was able to do so because it had been equipped with ASG radar, the kind that displayed returning echoes maplike on a plan position indicator scope. By the end of November 1942 all K-ships would have it. With radar, nighttime missions became practical.

Up until this time, airshipmen had had to rely on the eyeball and the magnetometer for finding U-boats. The chances of spotting one visually, however, were poor. The submarine could see the airship before the airship saw it and could dive in thirty seconds to escape detection.

The magnetometer in the magnetic anomaly detector (MAD) enabled a blimp to sense a submarine's presence. For security reasons the MAD was often called the marine airborne detector to conceal its principle of operation. It was a device that, in the opening months of the campaign against American shipping, the enemy knew

23

nothing about. Derived from the peacetime use of airplane-carried magnetometers for oil prospecting, MAD had been developed to "prospect" for U-boats. Daniel L. Humm, an electrical engineer with Columbia University's Airborne Instruments Laboratory, had been a technical leader in this work. After his death in a plane crash, a laboratory would be named for him at Lakehurst.*

MAD sensed a distortion or anomaly in the earth's magnetic field caused by the presence of a submarine. It had a vertical range through air or water of about four hundred feet, requiring the airship using it to fly below that height. To use MAD alone to look for a submarine in the ocean was like looking for the proverbial needle in the haystack. Probably worse. However, as a follow-up to a visual sighting or, later in the war, to a disappearing radar blip, the swing of the MAD's recorder needle could confirm that a U-boat was present. Or at least that a metallic body was.

Therein lay the rub. A submerged wreck could move the needle as readily as could a submarine. To distinguish, the pilot of a blimp equipped with MAD had to try to determine if the source of the magnetic signal was moving. He dropped a flare or bronze-powder marker where the signal had been received. Then he made repeated passes over the spot, similarly marking each successive signal. Sometimes he dropped an anchored yellow buoy as a marker. If the target was moving, a track was established. Release of bombs would follow. If the pilot lost contact, he would fly a circular or cloverleaf search pattern to try to regain it.

K-ships, in that first year of the war, carried four 325-pound Mark 17 depth bombs, two internally in a bomb bay under the cabin floor and two on outboard racks. Their Mark 24 hydrostatic fuzes had fifty-foot depth settings. To kill a U-boat, these bombs—*Wabos* the Germans called them—had to detonate within about forty-five feet of the submarine's pressure hull.

Meanwhile, other antisubmarine equipment was being developed, with Lakehurst's blimps serving as flying test platforms. These were the "Ls," *G-1*, and *K-2*. The ex-Army *TC-13* and *TC-14* were

---

* The author recalls being party in 1943 to a conversation in the Bureau of Aeronautics about a Russian request for K-ships. Suspecting, correctly or not, that what the Soviets really wanted was not the airships but the MAD equipment on board, the navy turned down the request.

no longer at Lakehurst, having been sent to California to form the nucleus of a West Coast operation.

One of these inventions was a small, expendable, air-droppable buoy, hydrophone- and radio-equipped, which picked up and transmitted the screw noises of a submarine. Called a "sonobuoy," it was destined to play a decisive role in the aircraft war against submerged U-boats.

A high-intensity underwater flare was also being tested. It was intended to reveal a submarine that passed between it and an observer overhead. The project was abandoned, but not before it led to tragedy on 8 June 1942. Two airships, the *G-1* and *L-2*, collided off Manasquan Inlet, New Jersey, while testing the flare. The night was dark but clear. The *G-1*, intentionally running without lights, turned in front of the other airship, which struck it. The crash caused the envelopes to split open and both blimps to fall to the water. Only one person survived, Ens. Howard S. Fahey, Jr., who would later be the author's roommate. Twelve men were killed, the first fatalities in airships in World War II. Among them were five scientists from Columbia University. The dead included one of LTA's most promising officers, Lt. Comdr. Clinton S. Rounds.

The crew of the *K-8*, Squadron Fourteen out of NAS Weeksville, came upon the enemy face to face on 9 July.* But in a lifesaving, not a combat, role. On the 7th an A-29, part of the army air force's antisubmarine effort, caught the *U-701* surfaced in broad daylight off Cape Hatteras and bombed and sank it. After two days the survivors, of whom there had been quite a few, had still not been found. The *K-8*, piloted by Ens. George S. Middleton, took off to look for them. Middleton assumed that the Gulf Stream had carried them some distance and set his course accordingly. His hunch proved correct. He saw an object in the water that turned out to be a man waving frantically to attract attention. Three more were nearby. All of them were oily and sunbaked, suffering severely from exposure. Several others had already died. Life jackets had kept them afloat. The airship's rubber life raft was dropped, and then a line lowered with food, water, a first-aid kit, a blanket, and a knife. The *K-8* reported its find. A Coast Guard Hall flying boat arrived in short

---

* To avoid confusing it with the Coast Guard Air Station Elizabeth City, the name of the naval air station at Elizabeth City was changed to Weeksville.

order, homing in on Middleton's radio transmissions. To assist the plane in landing and taking off, the airship dropped smoke bombs to show the direction of the wind. When the blimp suddenly spotted another group of three men, it marked their location. Seven of the U-boat's crew members were picked up, including Horst Degen, the captain. The *U-701* was the first enemy submarine bagged by aircraft off the Eastern Seaboard.

On 17 July the *K-3* of Squadron Fourteen dropped three Mark 17s upon a visible but unidentifiable underwater object, sighted while the airship was investigating an oil slick. The blimp had received MAD signals also, and the pilot judged the contact stationary or slightly moving. When he bombed it, up came more oil plus a lighter oil or gasoline, signs that the target was most likely a wreck.

The *K-9* lowers provisions to survivors of the *Moldanger*, torpedoed on 27 June 1942. These men were adrift for eighteen days before the airship found them. (U.S. Navy)

That same month the *K-9* was attracted by calls for assistance from an airplane circling two boatloads of survivors. Upon reaching the scene, the blimp lowered provisions and guided a PC boat to the rescue. The men were from the *Moldanger*, torpedoed by the *U-404* eighteen days earlier.

Blimps found two more boats with survivors in July. Lifesaving had, in fact, become so much a part of their operations that rescue kits were being carried. These kits contained water, emergency rations, a can opener, flares, a flashlight, and individual whiskies and chewing gum.

During the second half of 1942 German submarine activity dropped off in the patrol and escort areas of Squadrons Eleven, Twelve, and Fourteen. Dönitz had begun concentrating his boats more to the south, in the Gulf of Mexico, in the Caribbean, and even off Brazil, areas where antisubmarine defenses lagged those in the Eastern Sea Frontier and where, in the case of the Gulf and Caribbean, tanker traffic abounded. In May 1942 forty-one ships were lost to U-boats in the Gulf, forty-two during June and July in the Caribbean. There were sinkings in the approaches to the Panama Canal.

Although the enemy was scarcer, the blimps were becoming more numerous, continuing to escort and patrol. Two more "Ks" were delivered to squadrons in August and four more in September, months in which airships delivered five and three attacks, respectively.

In October an incident demonstrated the relative ease with which a slow-moving, even hovering, blimp could examine and identify an object in the water and the relative difficulty with which a heavier-than-air (HTA) craft could do the same. When a civil air patrol plane spotted what it considered a suspicious object and dropped smoke flares on it, a navy plane followed up with a bombing attack. There was an airship close at hand and it joined the party, quickly calling it to a halt because the blimp could see that the object being attacked was a clump of seaweed.

At Bar Harbor, Maine, an airship began operating at the beginning of October. At Cape May, New Jersey, another did the same on 14 October.

Also in October the *K-18* and *K-19* were flown to the newly activated Naval Air Station Richmond, Florida, about twenty miles

27

With operations expanding, squadrons began flying from South Weymouth, Massachusetts, and Weeksville, North Carolina. Here, a K-ship undocks from the steel hangar at Weeksville. (U.S. Navy)

southwest of Miami, to form Airship Patrol Squadron Twenty-One, which was commissioned there on 1 November. The new squadron would operate as part of the Gulf Sea Frontier. It would continue to report administratively to Commander Airship Patrol Group One until a new Group Two could be formed to consist of Squadron Twenty-One and the squadrons planned for Houma, Louisiana, and Hitchcock, Texas.

Airships delivered no attacks in November or December.

When the year ended, Squadron Twenty-One's two ships had made eighteen escort and fifty-seven patrol flights, logging 994 hours in the Gulf Sea Frontier. The thirteen airships of Squadrons Eleven, Twelve, and Fourteen in the Eastern Sea Frontier had flown 18,010 hours on 725 escort, 464 patrol, and 144 combined escort and patrol missions.

More than thirty attacks, all in daylight, had been delivered against presumed submarine contacts.*

* A search of the captured German naval archives by the author in 1946 showed little or no correlation between airship attacks and actions and what U-boat commanders reported in their logs. Blimps were observed by U-boat captains, one of them commenting that every time he put up his periscope for a look around, "the blimp was there." Another watched a K-ship through his scope, noting its details, which included the bombs on the outboard racks, the heavy machine gun in the turret, and a lighter machine gun in an after window. Flight reports for that day made no mention of any submarine having been sighted, although blimp and U-boat could not have been very far apart. According to a U.S. Navy survivor who had been torpedoed, picked up, and taken by the *U-402* back to St. Nazaire in May 1942, the crew mentioned they often saw blimps but submerged before the blimps could see the submarine.

3. THE KING SHIP

THE K-TYPE AIRSHIP was an elongated balloon inflated with helium. Its envelope was a three-ply bag of cotton fabric, impregnated with rubber or a synthetic substitute, neoprene, and coated on the inside with paraffin to discourage gas leakage. Neoprene was preferred. It suffered less deterioration under operating conditions, held gas better, and was not in such critically short wartime supply.

To the Bureau of Aeronautics, the aircraft was the ZNP-K, Z for lighter-than-air, N for nonrigid, P for patrol, and K for model or class. In the phonetic alphabet of the day, it was the Zebra Nan Peter King. Pilots called it the King ship.

In production it came in three sizes: 416 thousand, 425 thousand, and 456 thousand cubic feet. Almost as long as a city block, a K-ship's envelope fitted, when deflated, into a shipping box twelve feet long, six feet wide, and six feet high. Removed from the box—no easy task because the material weighed five tons—it was laid out on a protective ground cloth and covered with a net. After its fins were attached, inflation tubing was connected to it, and filling it with helium began. Each one thousand cubic feet of the gas produced a lift of about sixty-two pounds. As the bag filled up, it became increasingly buoyant, kept in place by the net, which was weighted down by sandbags. When the envelope was sufficiently full, the bus-length car was attached, the addition of its weight permitting the restraining net to be removed.

The pressure inside a K-ship's envelope was surprisingly low, the equivalent of one-and-a-half to two inches of water, or about one ounce of pressure per square inch. Small holes resulted in a slow leakage of helium and a gradual reduction of lift: nothing catastrophic. Larger punctures meant larger problems, but the "K's" ability to "take it" was remarkable. The *K-52*, for example, was

A K-ship at Kindley Field, Bermuda, on its way across the Atlantic. The air-transportable or expeditionary "stick mast," shown here, was widely used at advanced bases in lieu of the steel, mobile ones. (U.S. Navy)

returning from an all-night patrol and was still fifty miles from its base when the port engine cowling broke away, tearing a ten-inch and a seven-inch hole in the bag. Ens. Louis P. Reeder was nonetheless able to bring his ship home, an achievement that would earn him the Air Medal.

An air system that compensated for the expansion and contraction of the helium in flight or on the ground maintained pressure at

31

a constant level. Warmed by the sun, cooled by the rain, and subjected to different atmospheric pressures at different altitudes, the gas was constantly changing in volume. The air system responded to these changes by using inflatable chambers called ballonets, located fore and aft inside the envelope.

The two ballonets were about the same size. Together they equaled one-quarter of the total volume of the gas bag. The propeller slipstream was captured by means of a scoop in the leading edge of the engine outriggers. Then the air passed through dampers into a fabric air duct that led to the ballonets. Air entering through the portside damper was directed aft, air through the starboard side forward. By opening and closing these dampers with hand-pulled toggles and wires at the instrument panel, the pilot could control or "pump" the flow of air forward or aft.

Air has weight, of course, so its presence in the ballonets affected the ship's trim. More air forward than aft made the blimp nose heavy. Shifting air back and forth was how trim was managed. Also how it was mismanaged. Too much air forward could produce a condition that full-up elevator was hard put to overcome.

When the expanding helium pressed down on the ballonets, it squeezed air out of them through two automatic pressure valves, thirty-six inches in diameter. The vented air was exhausted through louvers in the upper sides of the car. Often these self-actuating valves did not open completely on their own, preferring to chatter and sing until the manual valve-control line in the cockpit was pulled and the air buildup released.

If the ballonets were empty—the altitude at which this took place was called "pressure height"—and the helium continued to expand, two twenty-inch-diameter automatic helium valves, located about halfway up either side of the envelope, relieved the overpressure. These valves opened when the gas pressure exceeded two-and-a-half to three inches of water. Like the air valves, the helium valves had wires running to them from toggles and wires at the pilot's station and could be operated manually. The intentional valving of helium was resorted to only in extremis.*

---

* To conserve helium, pilots tried to operate whenever possible below pressure height, which varied according to the amount and temperature of the gas in the bag. Usually, pressure height was well below five thousand feet. On patrol and escort, altitudes ranged between five hundred and one thousand feet, lower when MAD was being used to localize a contact.

The envelope, four thousand square yards in all, held the gas and was also the airship's prime structural member. Its strength depended on the firmness given it by the internal pressure of the gas.

Besides supporting the flight stresses, the envelope also carried the car. Four catenary curtains, running fore and aft in parallel rows, hung down on the inside from the top of the bag. Steel suspension cables connected the curtains to attachment points at the top of the car, the cables extending through the bag and emerging from its bottom through gastight sleeves. In addition to this internal suspension, there was an external attachment by which the roof of the car was secured to the bottom of the bag. The internal-suspension system carried about 90 percent of the load, the external 10 percent.

The car, forty-two feet long, fourteen feet high, and about nine feet wide, was made of chrome-molybdenum-steel tubing covered with sheet aluminum. In its later configurations, the entrance was

An interior view of a blimp envelope, in this case a postwar model, showing a catenary suspension curtain and a partially inflated air ballonet. (U.S. Navy 707915)

through double doors at the extreme aft end. Earlier models had a single starboard entrance door aft. Crews boarded or left the car via a five-foot metal ladder that was inserted in the doorway when the ship was on the ground and carried inboard over the door in flight. In the after end were a wash basin and a toilet, chairs for the off-duty crew, two canvas bunks swung up against the overhead, a single parachute for use in case someone had to jump to form up an emergency landing party, and the ship's inflatable yellow life raft. Individual life vests were carried but not parachutes. The low altitudes at which blimps flew, their slow speed, and their ability to absorb a crash impact like a giant, rubberized shock absorber, made parachutes unnecessary.

Forward on the starboard side were the gasoline-powered Lawrance auxiliary power unit, which provided additional electricity when needed, and the Homelite unit, which blew air into the ballonets when the prop wash was not sufficient. The crew could also blow air directly into the helium chamber as an emergency means of maintaining the pressure and form of the bag.

It is not difficult to tell who is on duty and who is not in this view of the aft end of a K-ship car. (U.S. Navy)

Mid-car, starboard side. (U.S. Navy)

Mid-car, port side. (U.S. Navy)

On the port side was the mechanic's station with its throttles, mixture controls, instruments, and dials. Forward of that were the radar display and the table where the navigator laid out his charts and worked his course. A small galley was also sandwiched in.

On the starboard side was the communications corner with its transmitters and receivers. K-ships trailed a lead-weighted antenna, something not generally known to the HTA types who sometimes liked to buzz and fly under the lumbering "poopy bags," as they called the blimps. There was never a collision between an airplane and an airship antenna wire and, as far as is known, no pilot ever tried to fly a loop around a blimp, no matter how much he might have wanted to. Nevertheless, the close approach of an airplane could give the crew of a K-ship some anxious moments.

The MAD contact indicator, the Esterline-Angus recorder with its swinging needle, was in the communications area, as were the sonobuoy receivers. Also in that general vicinity was the identification friend or foe (IFF) set, which sent a coded identifying signal, changed periodically, when triggered by an external radar. Headsets provided for communications between crew stations.

Overhead were eight aluminum fuel tanks, three forward and five aft, each capable of carrying 125 gallons of 91 octane aviation gasoline. The rearmost were fitted with dump valves so that fuel could be jettisoned. If fuel was dumped with little or no way on, such as during a landing, gasoline fumes could stay with, even envelop, the car, creating an extremely hazardous situation. Two other tanks, of one hundred gallons and eighty gallons, were located under the floor and could be released by the pilot. These slip tanks were a means of quickly getting rid of weight. Because of the many gasoline tanks in the car, no smoking was permitted.

The deck of the car was aluminum plating, patterned to prevent slipping. Balsa wood lay underneath. Deck panels gave access below the floor to the radar, slip tanks, landing wheel (cranked up and down by hand), and box housing the drag rope.

K-ships were damned noisy. There was no soundproofing, which would have added weight. It would have done little good anyway since the engines were just outside the windows and the windows

Sandbags, used for ballast on the ground, were taken off when weight, in this case chow, was put aboard. Heating in the early "Ks" was so poor that even the breakfast eggs froze. (U.S. Navy)

were often open. The Lawrance and Homelite units also generated a great racket inside the car. The price paid for a long patrol in a K-ship could be a ringing in the ears that lasted for hours.

The sense of smell was also affected. K-ships carried an aroma of rubber and aircraft dope.

In flight, K-ships rolled and pitched. Their behavior was more like a ship's than an airplane's.

Forward in the cockpit, the pilot and copilot sat side by side, with the pilot on the left. In front of them stretched a large wraparound Plexiglas or Lucite window area, giving an essentially unobstructed 180-degree view plus an ability to see straight down. Piloting a K-ship was a two-man job, particularly at low airspeeds when the rudders and elevators lost their "bite" and during landings in gusty conditions.

Flight duties were divided. Altitude was controlled from the left-hand side, course and heading from the right. To move the elevator surfaces on the horizontal fins, the pilot worked a twenty-two-inch wheel attached to the inboard (right) side of his seat. By turning it forward, he lowered the bow; to raise the bow, he turned the wheel backward. A foot brake helped him hold the wheel and elevators in position. He also had rudder pedals, but being extremely awkward to use, they seldom were.

The copilot on the opposite side steered, using a sixteen-inch wheel mounted like an automobile's on a column in front of him. Operating the rudders was like steering a boat. The airship's response was sluggish. A chain and sprocket drive transmitted turns of the rudder wheel, as of the elevator wheel, to control cables that exited through the after end of the car and ran externally beneath the underside of the bag to the control surfaces on the fins.

Brace cables, attached to the envelope with fabric patches, steadied and secured the four fins. They consisted of aluminum girderwork covered with doped cotton fabric. Before the war the K-ships' rudder and elevator surfaces had been painted with colorful red, white, and blue vertical stripes. Now the stripes were gone, replaced by aluminized or gray-colored dope. Similarly, the airship's number, "K-3," "K-4," or whatever, was no longer carried conspicuously on the side of the bag. Instead, it was painted in small characters high up on the side of the car. In addition, the American flag no longer flew from the stern.

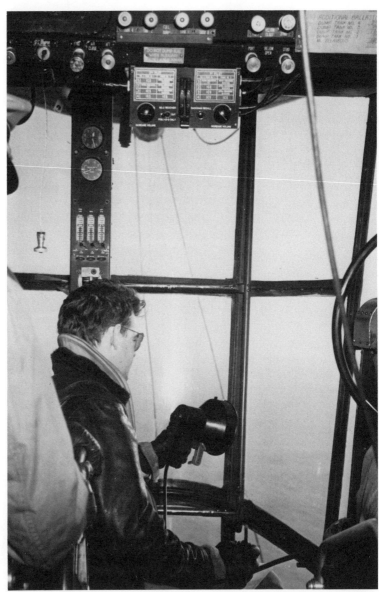

The crew member manning the flashing light is sitting in the bombardier's "well" between the pilot (left) and copilot (right). Above are the manually pulled toggles for the valves and dampers. The vertical arrangement of flight instruments before the pilot include three liquid manometers that indicate helium and air pressures inside the hull. (U.S. Navy)

The bottom fin was smaller than the others because K-ships customarily took off "heavy," their total or gross weight exceeding what their gas alone could lift. To overcome this heaviness, they made a take-off run on their wheel, becoming airborne when the aerodynamic lift generated by airspeed, angle of attack, and hull form overcame the heaviness. The reduced size of the lower stabilizer provided clearance so that, when the tail went down and the ship nosed up, the fin would not strike the ground. On its bottom edge it carried a small tail wheel or sometimes a skid. ZNP-Ks, although designed for a maximum "heavy" takeoff of 1,500 pounds, were commonly flown much heavier, 1,800, 2,000, even 3,000 pounds heavier than the lift that their helium alone would permit.

The bag was painted aluminum to reflect the heat of the sun and to minimize its effect on the gas inside. Camouflage had been attempted in prewar days with the *J-4*, which had been painted a robin's egg blue, and in 1942 with the *L-1*, which had been given a flat, bluish gray color. The results being inconclusive, it had been decided to leave well enough alone and stick with the aluminum pigment.

Hull reflectivity had much to do with the phenomenon known as "superheat." This was the difference in temperature between the outside air and the gas inside. On a clear hot day, with little or no wind, a K-ship on the mast could pick up as much as thirty to forty degrees Fahrenheit of superheat. Given the opposite weather conditions, the blimp would lose its heat. Thus, superheat could be positive or negative and, no matter which, substantially affect an airship's buoyancy.

Student pilots, in addition to being reminded again and again that using elevators and rudders moved the tail before the bow, were also driven to understand the nature and importance of superheat. Their parody of a popular radio jingle proved that they were getting the message. The jingle, a soap commercial, ran, "Super Suds, Super Suds, lots more suds from Super Suds." The LTA version, heard often being sung in the showers, was "Superheat, superheat, lots more lift from superheat." A superheat indicator, developed by the National Bureau of Standards, was mounted on the instrument panel in the cockpit.

This panel was in front of and above the heads of the pilot and copilot, its base even with the top of the window area. The location was inconvenient but not necessarily the result of poor design. It had been situated so as not to obstruct the cockpit's visibility. It met that stipulation alright, but the pilot needed a gorilla-like reach to get at the panel. Working the toggles and wires connected to the dampers and valves was often done standing up.

In front of the pilot were the instruments important to him as elevatorman: altimeter (barometric), vertical-speed indicator, elevator-angle indicator, manometers (which displayed the pressure in the helium chamber and air ballonets), and compass. They were arranged vertically in a small housing secured to the window frame. At night these and the other flight instruments glowed under ultraviolet lamps.

A sliding door closed off the cockpit area from the rest of the car. It was cozy inside with the pilot and copilot, the bombardier sitting on the deck between them, and the ordnanceman "upstairs" in the turret with his .50-caliber machine gun. The bombardier sat in something like a goldfish bowl with a curved Plexiglas window at his feet, a window that was frequently crushed. On one occasion a ground crewman, pushing hard against it, was surprised to find himself suddenly talking to the pilot from the inside instead of from the outside of the ship.

Penetrating the car fore and aft from the bag were two red manila ropes. These were the rip cords, the emergency means of deflating the ship completely and nearly instantaneously. Pulling them tore open two rip panels along the top of the envelope, allowing the helium to escape in a swift gush.

The twin engines were Pratt and Whitney R-1340-AN-2 Wasps of 550 horsepower each. (The *K-3* through *K-8* were powered by Wright engines.) These P and W power plants were operated downrated at 425 horsepower, out of consideration for the strength limits of the envelope. Their three-bladed, 12½ foot-diameter metal propellers were fixed in pitch during flight. Their settings could be adjusted or changed on the ground. On either side of the car was an access door to the engine nacelles. Hinged at the bottom, the doors lowered outboard into a kind of catwalk or work platform. Although they made it possible to reach the engines to repair them in flight, such repairs were seldom attempted.

In line with the propellers was a red vertical stripe: a reminder of an ever-present danger.

Forward of the engines and up on each side of the bag was an electronic head that contained the sensor for the MAD. The early "Ks" had carried it in a housing on the envelope's underside between the car and the bow mooring assembly.

Dangling from the bow were two sets of ground-handling ropes, a pair of short lines and a pair of long lines. The former, because they were too short to whip into the propellers, were allowed to trail and blow about in flight. The latter, long enough to entangle themselves with the blades, were stowed before takeoff in boxes, port and starboard, at the front of the car. The ground party used the short lines to hold the ship and keep it pointed into the wind after demasting and just prior to takeoff. The long lines were essentially landing ropes. Released and dropped as the blimp reached the handling party, they were caught hold of and used to slow the ship and, in the case of a "light" landing, to haul it down. For unusually light landings or those being made in high winds, a drag rope was also carried, stowed under the deck, to be dropped to the ground handlers if an additional line was needed. In good weather, ground handling required about forty men, more, of course, if it was bad, particularly if it was gusty.

Ram-air pressure required that the bow be reinforced by twenty-four battens, made of laminated spruce and individually covered with doped fabric. A bow cap of aluminum sheeting provided additional strength. These reinforcements resulted in such a rigid structure that at times, fortunately rare times, pressure on the bow would cause the bow cap to push back against the rest of the bag, creating great circumferential wrinkles. When the outside stress was relieved or internal pressure was increased, the nose would snap back into position and the wrinkles disappear. A Bureau of Aeronautics letter said that "large wrinkles may come and go without visible damage but they are a horrible sight."

A mooring cone, as well as a steel pendant or cable, hung from the tip of the bow. A line through the masthead would be connected to the cable and used to winch the ship up to the mast. The cone fitted into a masthead cup, which would be locked into position around it. The masts for K-ships, except for the concrete-embedded, guy-wired stick or expeditionary type, were red and white triangular structures mounted on wheels and pulled by tractors. These mobile masts were used for docking, undocking, and transporting the air-

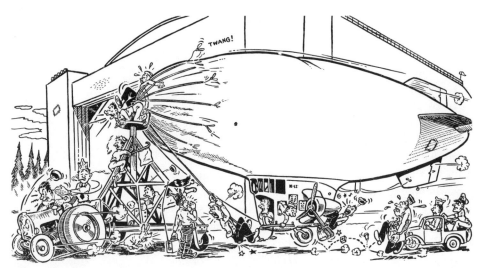

An eager-beaver ground-handling officer or speed-demon tractor driver could wreak havoc on a masted airship—as this cartoon by ZP-21's Bill Aldrin points out. (U.S. Navy)

ships to and from their mooring-out circles where, rolling on their landing wheels, they wind-vaned about their moorings. The masts were made of steel and electrically grounded by a length of chain. They had no brakes, relying on the tractors or on chocks to keep them in place. Otherwise they could roll about on their own. One midnight at South Weymouth a mast, pushed by fifty-to-sixty–knot winds, blew three hundred yards from the hangar door to the landing mat before being reined in.

The tractor drivers were among the most important persons on the field. They had in tow an aircraft with a mass of more than twenty-five thousand pounds. If they stopped abruptly or turned too suddenly or sharply, the blimp's momentum would keep it moving, with results that could include overriding the mast and puncturing the bag.

Even on the mast K-ships could act up and behave horribly. Wind flow over and around a hangar, superheat, or both could cause them to "kite," lifting their sterns high into the air and their cars well off the ground. Airships, when moored outside, had sandbags weighing thirty pounds on board for ballast. Even so, they sometimes kited eighty degrees, standing virtually on their noses.

Nothing, however, could match an airship's aversion to an inversion, that meteorological condition in which low-lying air is colder than the air above. Trying to land a blimp in an inversion could be unmitigated hell. LTA vehicles fly according to the Principle of Archimedes, deriving their lift from the weight of the air they displace. The colder the air, the greater its density and its weight.

When an airship descends into colder air to land, its lift increases, a self-defeating state of affairs, to say the least. The problem is worse if the ship happens to be "light," having burned off its original heaviness by consuming fuel. Getting down by valving helium was strongly disapproved of to conserve the gas and to keep from having to replenish it or top off what remained. So landing approaches had to be made and repeated until, flying nose down to generate negative aerodynamic lift, the ship eventually came low enough to the ground

A "light" landing, in which the airship had to be driven aerodynamically to the ground, could be a landing to remember. (U.S. Navy)

to place its handling lines, car rail, and drag rope into the hands of the awaiting and long-suffering ground crew. When forcing itself down, it had to have a fair amount of airspeed, but to permit the ground party to grab the lines, it had to slow down. When it did, it began to rise again. One exhausted ground-handling officer reportedly broke down on the field and cried, frustrated beyond all understanding by an airship's unwillingness to come down. It was said at Lakehurst that one K-ship had made thirteen attempts before getting down. A South Weymouth airship was reputed to have made something like nineteen!

During an early ferry flight from Lakehurst to Richmond, Florida, the pilot of a K-ship dutifully kept the NAS Jacksonville tower informed of his position, calling in and reporting what must have seemed like glacial progress compared to other aircraft in the area. One of the controllers, mystified by this slow-moving vehicle, finally demanded, "Say, what kind of aircraft are you anyway?"

This is the kind of aircraft the K-ship was.

4. REACHING STRENGTH

PLANNED IN 1940, implemented in 1941, and made operational in 1942, the LTA buildup continued in 1943.

Squadron Fifteen came on line on 1 February 1943 at Naval Air Station Glynco, Georgia. There was no place by that name. The closest town to the base was Brunswick. It would have been appropriate to name the station Brunswick, but there already was a Naval Air Station Brunswick, Maine. To avoid having two naval air stations named Brunswick, the navy called the Georgia site Glynco for Glynn County, in which it was located.

The squadron's first commanding officer was Comdr. John D. Reppy. Thin, slight in build, and red-haired, he had served aboard the *Macon* and had reportedly been the last man off before it sank beneath the surface of the Pacific. Squadron Fifteen began its operations with two wooden hangars that had not yet been completed and with no bachelor officers quarters. Because a fire had destroyed the BOQ, pilots were housed at the King and Prince, a resort hotel on St. Simons Island, a temporary measure no one objected to in the least.

Squadron Fifteen was the southernmost airship squadron in the Eastern Sea Frontier. The next down the coast was Twenty-One in the Gulf Sea Frontier. Comdr. Gerald D. Zurmuehlen had assumed command of Twenty-One when it was commissioned on 1 November 1942. Zurmuehlen, whose outgoing personality and keen wit made him one of the most personable of all LTA unit commanders, relinquished this assignment to take command of Squadron Fifty-One, commissioned on 10 February 1943 to be based in Trinidad.

The fifteenth of May was start-up day for Squadron Twenty-Two at NAS Houma. "Fighting John" McCormick arrived from Squadron Eleven to be Twenty-Two's commanding officer until 4

Throughout the war Naval Air Station Lakehurst, New Jersey, would be the hub of navy LTA activity. Squadron Twelve airships operated out of Hangars #5 and #6 in the foreground. Station blimps engaged in training and experimental flights, and those undergoing assembly and repair were housed in the hangars on the far side of the field. Commander Fleet Airships, Atlantic was headquartered here, as was the Chief of Naval Airship Training and Experimentation. (U.S. Navy)

October, when he was relieved by the first naval reservist to command an airship squadron, Lt. Comdr. Raymond C. Gossom.

Perhaps it was McCormick . . . or the local Louisiana hot sauce . . . or the heat and humidity of Terrebonne Parish . . . or the hangar with its special doors . . . Squadron Twenty-Two and Houma (pronounced Hō-ma) were always looked upon as being a bit different.

Its aircrews claimed that their thunderstorms were the fiercest. Its ground crews bragged that their mosquitoes were the biggest. The squadron gave names to its airships, an uncommon practice in LTA. To be sure, Twenty-One had its "Dopey" (*K-17*), "Marauder" (*K-40*), and "Acey Deucey" (*K-53*), and Twelve had its "Jersey Bounce." Only Twenty-Two went about selecting names on a methodical basis, however, naming its airships for the local pirates of bygone days. That is how its *K-54* became the "Jean La Fitte," its

K-56 the "Dominique You," and its *K-57* the "Nez Coupé" (so called because its progenitor had been parted from his proboscis during a vintage saber duel). A fourth airship was called the "Gambi." These were fitting names indeed. Every day the squadron's pirate fleet used old Fort Livingstone as a navigational landmark. Livingstone stood on the site of La Fitte's Grande Terre hangout of over a century before.

La Fitte, Dominique You, and the others had been real-life characters. Not satisfied with them, Squadron Twenty-Two set about creating a make-believe one, the fictitious airshipman Hogan Heliumhead. He was Dilbert's LTA counterpart, Dilbert being the car-

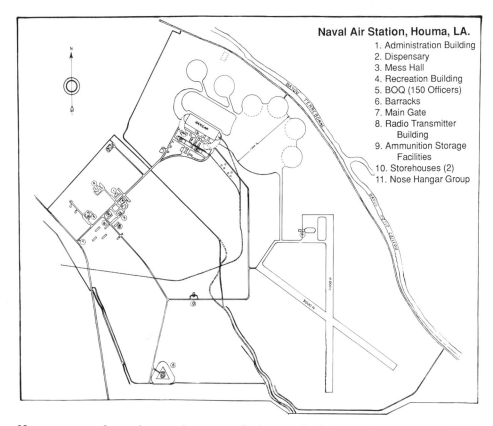

Naval Air Station, Houma, LA.
1. Administration Building
2. Dispensary
3. Mess Hall
4. Recreation Building
5. BOQ (150 Officers)
6. Barracks
7. Main Gate
8. Radio Transmitter Building
9. Ammunition Storage Facilities
10. Storehouses (2)
11. Nose Hangar Group

Houma, except for its hangar doors, was fairly typical of the naval air stations (LTA) built along the coasts. (U.S. Navy)

toon character invented by the Bureau of Aeronautics to personify the heavier-than-air pilot "who didn't know any better" and who broke every safety rule in the book. Hogan started out as an enlisted man but soon worked his way up to pilot and officer rank. He was drawn by W. D. Eubank, an aviation machinist's mate third class.

With all this creative thinking going on, Twenty-Two must have had a tremendous squadron insignia. Alas, if it did, no copy seems to have survived. Considering the squadron's location, you can bet that logo would have featured a pelican.

In many ways the squadron at Houma was ingenious. Take recognition training, for example. Pilots were expected to study pictures, silhouettes, and drawings of ships and aircraft so that they could identify the real thing when they saw it. Getting their attention long enough to teach them was a real challenge to the air combat intelligence (ACI) officer who was responsible for that training. The squadron ACI man at Houma hit upon the solution one day when he happened to read, "Objects glimpsed in moments of stress are indelibly impressed on the mind." Taking a cue from this pithy statement, he proceeded to mount his recognition posters in the "head" on the inside of the stall doors—and his ingenuity met with training results beyond all expectations.

Just as no record of Squadron Twenty-Two's insignia seems to have survived, so there is none of any mascot. Perhaps this was why Ens. Donald C. Sandow, Jr., and crew were happy that a duck joined them when they were ninety miles at sea and flew formation with the blimp all the way to the coast. Spirits brightened on what had otherwise been an uneventful and uninteresting mission. Here, perhaps, was a future squadron mascot on the wing. Feathered friend, however, headed off on its own upon reaching land. All the airship crew had to show for the experience were pictures they took of the bird flying alongside, thirty feet away.

The bayou climate, the cumulonimbi, the clouds of bugs, and the colorful airship names were truly distinctive. But what really set operations at Houma apart—and teeth to gnashing—were the hangar doors. Instead of sill-mounted sectional sliding doors, the ones at Houma opened by moving along railroad tracks to the side of the structure. In the open position they were completely separate from the building itself. To the airshipmen at Houma who had to put up with these unconventional doors and the difficulties of making

The hangar at Houma, Louisiana, famous or infamous for its detachable doors. (U.S. Navy)

them work, these examples of the handiwork of the Bureau of Yards and Docks, the designer and builder, were the "BuDocks Folly." As pointed out earlier, the doors were necessary because the load-bearing properties of the soil could not support the weight of the usual type.*

The next squadron to begin operating was Twenty-Three, commissioned on 15 June 1943 at Naval Air Station Hitchcock, Texas. The squadron commander was Michael F. D. Flaherty. Hitchcock lay just a few miles northwest of the important oil port of Galveston.

Also on the 15th Squadron Forty-One, which in its early planning stages had been identified as Fifty-Two, was established. It would be based along the northeastern coast of Brazil. Lt. Comdr.

* On 21 April 1944 these separable doors led to catastrophe. With the southeastern door inoperative and stuck full open, fifty-five–knot winds entered the hangar, blew open the opposite door, and swept the *K-56, K-57,* and *K-62* from their tie-downs. Out through the northwestern end they sailed, the *K-56* deflating in the trees, the *K-57* crashing, exploding, and burning in a potato patch, and the *K-62* catching fire after striking power lines. No one was on board. No one was injured.

49

Daniel M. Entler was the commanding officer. Entler, like a number of other career-conscious officers of the Regular Navy, considered duty in airships a dead end and transferred to HTA flight training.

On 15 July 1943 the Atlantic Fleet airship organization was changed: the operating squadrons would be grouped into Fleet Airship Wings One, Two, Four, and Five and numbered 11, 12, 14, 15, 21, 22, 23, 41, 42, and 51 accordingly. They also underwent a name change from airship patrol squadron to blimp squadron. The two earlier airship patrol groups were abolished and replaced by the wings.

To enable the blimp squadrons to concentrate on flight operations, a new type command called a blimp headquarters squadron assumed the maintenance functions. There were four of these, each numbered identically with the wing that it served and each with detachments located wherever the blimp squadrons of that wing were based.*

The type commander, responsible for administering the airship activities of the Atlantic Fleet, would continue to be George H. Mills, headquartered at Lakehurst. His new title would be Commander Fleet Airships, Atlantic (ComFairshipsLant) and his new rank commodore. For six months, since December 1942, Mills had been Commander Fleet Airship Wing Thirty, which included the two airship patrol groups covering the Eastern and Gulf Sea Frontiers. As group and then wing commander, Mills had had the assistance of an exceptionally able chief staff officer, Lt. Comdr. Douglas L. L. Cordiner. All business, no-nonsense, somewhat humorless, yet personally understanding of "wet behind the ears" ensigns like the writer, Cordiner would transfer to destroyer duty in 1944, go on to HTA flight training, and later pilot the first plane to land at the South Pole.

On 1 September Blimp Squadron Forty-Two, was commissioned under Comdr. Charles L. Werts preparatory to moving to South America, where it would operate from the bulge of Brazil to Rio de Janeiro.

At Lakehurst, meanwhile, a major new entity had come into being on 15 May 1943: the Naval Airship Training and Experimental

---

* Although BlimpRon and BlimpHedRon were the official abbreviations for these new units, they were often written as blimpron and blimphedron, in actual practice. The blimprons were also known as ZPs and will usually be referred to as such in the remainder of this narrative.

A result of the Houma doors: the *K-62* after being blown out of the hangar and into a power line. (U.S. Navy)

Command (NATEC). The Chief of Naval Airship Training and Experimentation was Rear Adm. Charles E. Rosendahl, just back from the Pacific, where he had commanded the USS *Minneapolis* in action against the Japanese in the Battle of Tassafaronga on 30 November 1942. Although his cruiser had been severely damaged, he was able to save it. He had been awarded the Navy Cross for "extraordinary heroism" and promoted.

Rosendahl lived, breathed, and personified airships. He had served aboard the *Shenandoah*, had been the senior surviving officer aboard when she broke apart in 1925, and with others had free ballooned her forward section to a safe landing. By act of Congress he had received the Distinguished Flying Cross. Command of the *Los Angeles* (1926–29) and of the *Akron* (1931–32) followed. In 1928 he was the navy's observer on the *Graf Zeppelin's* first flight across the North Atlantic and was aboard that German airship in a similar role when she circled the globe the following year.

After commanding the *Akron*, Rosendahl had gone to sea aboard

51

Rear Adm. Charles E. Rosendahl and Capt. George H. Mills escort the governor of New Jersey, Charles Edison, through one of the new wood-and-concrete hangars at Lakehurst. Edison, son of the inventor, had been supportive of LTA craft as secretary of the navy and had brought Rosendahl to Washington to plan the coming wartime expansion. At the war's end, Edison would unsuccessfully urge Rosendahl to enter New Jersey politics. (U.S. Navy)

the battleship *West Virginia* and then the heavy cruiser *Portland.* Then, in June 1934, he had returned to Lakehurst as the station's commanding officer. He had held that command when the *Hindenburg* burned there in 1937. Duty as executive officer aboard the light cruiser *Milwaukee* followed, from September 1938 to May 1940. Then he reported to Washington, D.C., and to the Secretary of the Navy Charles Edison as his advisor on airships. Edison, who was favorably disposed toward airships, left almost immediately to run successfully for governor of New Jersey, being succeeded as secretary by the Chicago newspaper publisher Frank Knox. Rosendahl stayed on in the Office of the Chief of Naval Operations and in the Bureau of Aeronautics as a special assistant for LTA matters. As such, he had much to do with the immediate prewar planning for the buildup in airships, bases, personnel, and helium production. One of his major contributions had been selecting the coastal sites where the new LTA stations were to be built. In the summer of 1942 he had been ordered to the Pacific and to command of the *Minneapolis.*

Rosendahl was the navy's best-known airshipman, indeed the nation's. His books *Up Ship!* (1931) and *What About the Airship?* (1938) and his many public appearances, speeches, and articles advocating the airship's cause, had made him a popular, even heroic, figure.

When "Rosie" returned from the Pacific, the navy probably did not quite know what to do with him. The two top operational commands, Fleet Airships, Atlantic and Fleet Airships, Pacific already had commanders, the one a commodore, the other a captain. Rosendahl, a rear admiral, was probably considered too senior for either assignment. So a special one was created for him: Chief of Naval Airship Training and Experimentation.

Under his direction, airship training would henceforth be divided into a basic course, offered at NAS Moffett Field, California, and an advanced course, offered at Lakehurst. Pilot trainees had to master the usual subjects of any flight syllabus, plus aerostatics, the science of LTA flight, a science built upon the properties and behavior of gases. Experience gained flying L-, G-, and K-type airships would reinforce classroom-acquired knowledge. Flights were also made in free balloons, mostly thirty-five thousand cubic footers, to give potential pilots a firsthand feel for the motions and dynamics of the atmosphere, also to prepare them for the possibility of having to keep in the air or land an airship without power. Because the gas of

Primary LTA flight training was given in these L-ships at NAS Moffett Field in California. Advanced training was in K-ships at Lakehurst. (U.S. Navy)

a free balloon was released at the end of the flight, and because helium was not to be wasted, training was done in hydrogen-filled balloons.

Upon completing their flight training, students were designated naval aviators (airship) and awarded their wings of gold, identical to the wings worn by their HTA brethren.* In 1941 the navy had one hundred pilots qualified or in the process of qualifying in airships. In 1944 it would have 1,500. Enlisted airship aircrewmen would increase in number from one hundred to three thousand in the same period. Training airships at Moffett and Lakehurst flew 280 thousand hours during the war.

Rosendahl's interests were limitless and so, too, were the experi-

* As a carryover from earlier times, some officers in LTA wore half-wings, a sign they were checked out or qualified only in balloons.

ments and developments undertaken under his auspices. Bow elevators for airships, air/sea rescue hoists, electric propellers, even the carrying and release of a small plane were pursued.

Rosendahl wore two stars and Mills one. Lakehurst was not used to having two flag officers, or even one, on board. Rosendahl's being a shore command, he and his wife, Jean, lived on station in the red-brick Quarters "A." Mills, heading a Fleet activity, had his headquarters on station but, with wife, Lee, and daughter, Georgia Lee, rented a house in the town of Toms River about ten miles away. LTA was a small pond and "Rosie" and "Shorty" two rather sizable frogs. How would they get along?

They did just fine. From the start it was evident that they respected each other. To Rosendahl's credit, higher ranking and bigger cheese that he was, he tried not to get involved or interfere with the operations ongoing in the Fleet. That was Mills's business, and

Primary flight training included free ballooning. (U.S. Navy)

Rosendahl left him pretty much alone. What interested "Rosie" was the politics of airships, particularly on the Washington scene. Mills, aware of that, stayed out of his way in such matters.

As the champion and defender of the airship faith, Rosendahl was very effective. He was an impressive and attractive figure, tall and erect, his blue eyes and strong chin reflecting his Scandinavian forebears. He had that characteristic known as "command presence." He was articulate and his voice clear and authoritative. Obviously a man who knew what he wanted, what he wanted was airships. He fought for them with inexhaustible energy and zeal. In doing so, he frequently ruffled feathers, sometimes important ones.

"Rosie" played hardball. When he learned that airships were being bad-mouthed at the Air Combat Intelligence Officers School at Quonset Point, Rhode Island, he picked up the phone without hesitation, called its commanding officer, and was overhead by the author to chew him out with these words: "I do not understand how you can presume to criticize what is an established part of the United States Fleet. I am to see Admiral King tomorrow and can assure you that this matter will be at the top of my agenda." Some months later an officer from Lakehurst was by happenstance at Quonset and not by happenstance partaking of a restorative at the officers club. A barstool acquaintance, upon hearing that he came from Lakehurst, asked him if he could shed any light on "the big flap" that had involved airships, the Commander-in-Chief, U.S. Fleet and Chief of Naval Operations (King had both jobs), and the removal, so he said, of the school's commanding officer.

Rosendahl and Ernie King were friends, although nobody seemed to know how close or for how long. There were various times in which they could have gotten to know each other. King, an HTA aviator, had been Assistant Chief of the Bureau of Aeronautics (1928–29) and Chief (1933–36) after Admiral Moffett was killed on the *Akron*. Some said King and Rosendahl could not help having known each other, considering how many times they must have met coming in or out of Navy Department offices, each buttonholing anyone who might be able to help him achieve his goal: in King's case, selection to command the U.S. Fleet; in Rosendahl's, support for airships.

Rosendahl had some of King's well-known characteristics. He could be stiff and autocratic. Mills, in contrast, was relaxed and casual.

Mills wore regulation khakis on inspection trips. Rosendahl did, too, when he started out, but before arriving in his Lockheed R50 Lodestar, he would change into a tailored tropical worsted.

Commodore Mills was also assigned an R50 and, before that, a small Lockheed Electra of special design known as an XR20. It was in a civil version of the XR20 that Amelia Earhart disappeared in 1937.

The admiral's pilot was Pat Brett. A former enlisted man who was then a lieutenant commander, he had a mustache and was suave and handsome, reminding some of the matinee idol Jack Holt.

Halbert E. Leedom, the commodore's pilot, was short, a bit on the rumpled side, and, like Brett, a former enlisted aviation pilot. A happy-go-lucky type, Leedom was an exceptional flier, saving the XR20 one day when its landing gear began collapsing during touch-down and later intentionally ground-looping, without damage, the R50 to keep it from running out of field on Cuba's Isle of Pines.

"Hal" Leedom, a lieutenant when the author knew him, had been Admiral King's personal pilot when King was Chief of the Bureau of Aeronautics. Leedom liked to tell stories about King, particularly about his penchant for showing up unexpectedly at some unsuspect-ing air station at 0800 when everybody was supposed to be at work. After instructing Leedom to park the plane where he should not—King wanted to see if the rules were enforced—he would get out and stand looking at his pocket watch, timing how long it would take for his presence to be acknowledged. While waiting, he would stop passersby, officer and enlisted, and dress them down for being out of uniform, needing a haircut, or perhaps simply walking in an unmilitary manner. Then he would line them all up by the plane while they waited for the duty officer or commanding officer to show up.

There were other airplanes besides the two R50s at Lakehurst, planes like the stagger-wing Beech and the low-wing, two-seat, util-ity SNJ. There were also other aviators to fly members of Rosen-dahl's and Mills's staffs to Washington, D.C., Norfolk, and the var-ious blimp bases. One of the most common runs was to NAS Norfolk, headquarters of Air Force, Atlantic Fleet. The AirLant staff had an airship officer regularly assigned to it: Lt. Comdr. Charles E. Becker and, later, Comdr. Willard M. Hanger.

A frequent commuter around the airship circuit was a Naval Reserve lieutenant, Walter F. Zepke, the Engineering Officer of Fleet

Airships, Atlantic. In civilian life he had been with Pratt and Whitney. The K-ship's engines were his meat. He knew them backwards and forwards, hot and cold, running and not running. Because the R-1340-AN-2s suffered frequently from stuck exhaust valves—the result of the low engine speeds used while loitering or hovering—he was constantly on the go, answering calls for help from the blimp headquarters squadrons and their detachments. Zepke, short in stature, was of European origin, but just where in Europe no one seemed to know. He spoke with a German-like accent and had difficulty pronouncing the letter "V." When he talked about valves, he called them "walws." As "Stuck Valve" Zepke, he was known everywhere that K-ships were flying.

Akron, home of Goodyear Aircraft, was, of course, constantly visited. In June 1942 Public Law 612 had increased the navy's authorized airship strength to two hundred. This enabled more airships to be contracted for, but the number ordered was short of the number authorized. Change orders, design improvements, spare parts, costs, and scheduling were matters handled between the navy and Goodyear through the resident Bureau of Aeronautics representative, the BAR, who was Capt. Cornelius V. S. Knox. "Connie" Knox had performed a similar function in a more junior role as a member of the Inspector of Naval Aircraft's office during the building of the *Akron* and *Macon* in the late 1920s and early 1930s.

K-cars were assembled production-line style on the hangar deck inside the Goodyear airdock built originally for the *Akron* and *Macon*. Then the world's largest building without internal supports, it measured 1175 × 200 × 325 feet. In addition to airship cars, Goodyear would produce four thousand gull-wing FG Corsair fighter planes there.

In the Goodyear Balloon Room in Plant #1, workers, mostly women, made the envelopes, lapping, cementing, sewing, and taping their seams. They wore canvas shoes to keep from scuffing and puncturing the material when they walked on it.

The last of the ZNP-Ks produced by Goodyear was the *K-135*. Altogether, beginning with the *K-2*, the company had built 134 of the type. It had assembled and delivered 102 to Lakehurst. For Pacific Fleet operations, three had been flown cross-country from Akron to the West Coast. Twenty-nine more were shipped to NAS Moffett Field, California, and assembled there. Peak production was in May 1943, when eleven were completed.

During K-ship production, cars and envelopes were trucked out of town to Wingfoot Lake, home base of the Goodyear advertising blimps, for final assembly. The Wingfoot shed, the same one used in World War I, held three "Ks" at a time. Before being delivered to the navy, K-ships had to spend four hours in the air to have their instruments calibrated and their flight performance verified. Goodyear pilots under Karl Fickes, Director of Flight Operations, flew the ships, usually over Lake Erie, with representatives of the company's Flight Test Department and the navy BAR office present.

In addition to the 134 K-ships, Goodyear also built four M-ships,

The navy's wartime airship fleet: the L-, G-, K-, and M-types. Proportionally in scale. (U.S. Navy)

ten L-ships, and seven G-ships. The Bureau of Aeronautics classified these as ZNP-Ms, ZNN-Ls, and ZNN-Gs, the second "N" in the L- and G-ship series signifying training. According to the bureau, the average cost of a "K," "M," "G," or "L" was about $299 thousand, $707 thousand, $157 thousand, and $91 thousand, respectively.

The first "M," which was delivered to Lakehurst in November 1943, had a volume of 625 thousand cubic feet. The *M-2, M-3,* and *M-4,* sequentially delivered in January, February, and April 1944, were 647,500 cubic footers. Subsequently, all were increased to 725 thousand cubic feet. With their impressive volume, roughly half-again larger than that of a "K," the "Ms" were intended to operate in the tropics, where the warm and less dense air would generate less lift per cubic foot. Twenty-two were planned, but only four were built. The U-boat threat had diminished, and the "Ks" were proving themselves capable of almost any airship mission assigned.

M-ships—the larger ones were about 310 feet long—were notable for innovations. Instead of two ballonets, they had four, two amidships and one in either end. The center ones were interconnected to act as one, making it possible to use them to compensate for altitude changes while reserving the others for trimming. The "Ms" had the same Pratt and Whitney Wasp engines as did the "Ks." In flight the Curtiss electric propellers of the "Ms" were controllable in pitch and reversible. The K-ships' props were not. On the M-ship, the air scoops, bomb bay doors, and retractable landing gear were hydraulically operated.

The M-ships' car was 117 feet in length, built in three articulated sections, with a large "blister" for a machine gun underneath. The length of the car, unusual for a blimp, was designed to distribute weight and minimize stresses. Suspension loads were fairly evenly divided between the internal catenaries and cables and the external car attachment system at the bottom of the bag.

The *M-1* was based at Lakehurst. Because it was reserved for experimentation, it became the *XM-1.* Its accomplishments included carrying and dropping a Piper Cub in flight. The other "Ms" were assigned to Squadron Twenty-One at Richmond, Florida. Good airships that provided good performance, their few numbers never really gave them the opportunity to show what they could do.

The closest any "M" came to engaging the enemy occurred at Lakehurst at the end of a ferry flight from Richmond. Metro-

Goldwyn-Mayer was filming *This Man's Navy* with Wallace Beery. The film included such Beeryisms as a fist fight in a balloon and his piloting of a K-ship under attack by Japanese airplanes over the jungles of Burma. For filming the sequences showing the enemy planes, navy SNJs were painted with Japanese colors and flown around the air station. Along came the M-ship. The pilot and crew, however, knew nothing about the making of the movie or about the "enemy" aircraft. One can imagine their consternation when they suddenly saw a formation of planes with Japanese markings suddenly shoot by. General quarters was sounded, and those on board prepared for the worst, which fortunately was not forthcoming.

The L-ships were standard Goodyear advertising blimps. They were small: 123 thousand cubic feet, 149 feet long, and powered by two 145-horsepower Warner R-500-2/6 engines. There would be a total of twenty-two of them.

Goodyear had delivered three—the *L-1, L-2,* and *L-3*—to Lakehurst before the outbreak of the war. When hostilities began, the navy purchased Goodyear's advertising fleet, which consisted of five blimps. The *Resolute* became the *L-4*, the *Enterprise* the *L-5*, the *Reliance* the *L-6*, the *Rainbow* the *L-7*, and the *Ranger* the *L-8*. The *L-7* was assigned to Lakehurst, the others to Moffett Field. At Moffett, four more were built, using Goodyear-built envelopes and cars fabricated in the air station's shops. The remaining ten were contracted for with Goodyear, which used a subcontractor, Flexible Coach in Loudonville, Ohio, to produce the cars. The navy had its full complement of L-ships before the end of 1943. They were used for training and, for a time on the West Coast before the arrival of the "Ks," for patrol.

The *ZNN-G*, 196,700 cubic feet in volume and 192 feet long, was close enough to the size and design of the prewar *G-1* to warrant its inclusion under the "G" designation. Seven were ordered from Goodyear, which again employed as a subcontractor another bus manufacturer, Twin Coach of Kent, Ohio, to build the cars. The *G-2* through *G-8*, powered by twin 220-horsepower Continental R-670-6 engines, were delivered between September 1943 and February 1944.

So it went, a buildup in airships, bases, flight crews, and ground-support personnel, most of it for Atlantic Fleet operations, some of it for training, and some for Pacific Fleet operations.

Some LTA "brass": (left to right) Rosendahl; unidentified; Charles H. Kendall, Commander Squadron Twelve; unidentified; "Fighting John" McCormick; Mills; and Douglas Cordiner, Mills's chief staff officer. (U.S. Navy)

Not all of this expansion was the navy's, however. The Department of Interior's Bureau of Mines played a major part by taking steps to increase its production of helium. It already had a plant operating in Amarillo, Texas, and it built four more: the Exell, near Amarillo, named for a cattle brand; the Otis, in Kansas; another in Kansas at Cunningham; and the Navajo plant at Shiprock, New Mexico. In four years America's production of the inert gas leaped from 10 million to 137 million cubic feet a year. As it turned out, this was much more than was needed.

5. CONTACTS AND ATTACKS

K-SHIPS ENTERED THE hostilities with Mark 17 depth bombs, which were gradually replaced by the Marks 44 and 47. Torpex-filled, these newer 350-pounders had Mark 224 and 234 fuzes, which could be set for 25-, 50-, 75-, 100-, and 125-foot depths. Twenty-five feet or fifty feet was the usual setting. Like the Mark 17, these bombs had a lethal radius of about forty-five feet against U-boats then in service.

Later, airship squadrons operating in submarine-active areas, Squadrons Eleven at South Weymouth and Twelve at Lakehurst, for example, would be supplied with Mark 24 mines. The Mark 24 was not a mine at all but an acoustic torpedo. Much larger and heavier than any airship depth bomb, it was 7 feet long and 17 inches in diameter, weighed 680 pounds, and packed 92 pounds of HBX-1 explosive. It homed on a submarine's cavitation, the forming and then collapsing of the partial vacuums created by the rotating blades of the screws. It could chase the source for ten minutes at twelve knots. Because a surfaced U-boat could outrace it, the weapon's usefulness was for underwater attack after sonobuoys had detected the submarine. Blimp crews listened to records of cavitation when training to use the torpedo. Watched over by armed guards and kept shrouded by tarpaulins, the Mark 24 was known by the code name Mickey Mouse.

In addition to depth bombs and, beginning in 1944, the Mark 24 "mine," other airship ordnance included a .50-caliber Browning aircraft machine gun in a turret above the pilot and copilot positions and a smaller .30-caliber in one of the car's after windows. The .50-caliber, which could fire from the near-horizontal to eighty-five degrees below the horizon, could also rake targets at up to sixty degrees to either side of dead ahead. Set in an adapter that positioned the weapon and absorbed recoil, it had an illuminated sight, backed up by a standby ring sight in case of electrical failure. The gunner had four magazines, each holding sixty rounds of tracer and armor-piercing ammunition.

K-ships communicated via three receivers and one low- and one medium-power transmitter. The frequencies used ranged between 195 and 9050 kilocycles. Transmissions were by voice and continuous wave (CW) to a maximum range of about five hundred miles. In CW, now almost a lost art, a carrier wave was modulated by a telegraph key into the dots and dashes of the Morse code. Because merchant ships were not equipped for voice radio, airships used CW, visual signaling, shouting (when the engines were idling), or message drops to communicate. Sometimes a surface vessel observ-

A K-ship dropping a depth bomb. (U.S. Navy)

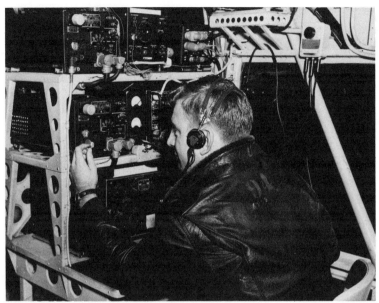

The radio shack. (U.S. Navy)

ing radio silence would blinker a message for a blimp to relay to shore. Squadron Twenty-One's *K-85* must have set some kind of record when, after agreeably saying, "Glad to," found itself on the receiving end of an eighty-five group—five letters to a group—encoded text sent to it by flashing light.

For secure communications to the base, carrier pigeons were sometimes used. The requirements, of course, were a fixed base, trained birds, and a cote. Lakehurst had a fine brood, capably tended by the station's pigeon quartermaster. South Weymouth's loft had 364 birds.

Releasing pigeons from airships in flight had to be done carefully to avoid injuring them. They were set free from the extreme aft end of the car to keep them as far as possible away from the propeller slipstream. So that they would not strike the fin surfaces and bracing wires, they were grasped firmly with wings closed and thrown downward. Taking wing, they would circle and then head for the base. There were stories, of course, of birds that chose to ride home on the upper fin rather than fly back on their own.

For navigating the civil airways and homing on their bases, airships had the radio aids of the day. South Weymouth typically maintained communication with its Blimp Squadron Eleven (ZP-11) airships on a patrol frequency of 3475 kilocycles.

There were more blimps in service in 1943 but fewer U-boats in their operating areas. By the time Blimp Squadrons Twenty-Two (ZP-22) and Twenty-Three (ZP-23) settled in at Houma and Hitch-

For communicating with base while observing radio silence, pigeons were sometimes carried (above). The birds had to be carefully released (top right) to prevent the prop wash and tail assembly from injuring them. Air stations having airships and pigeons naturally also had to have a cote like this one (right) at Lakehurst. (U.S. Navy)

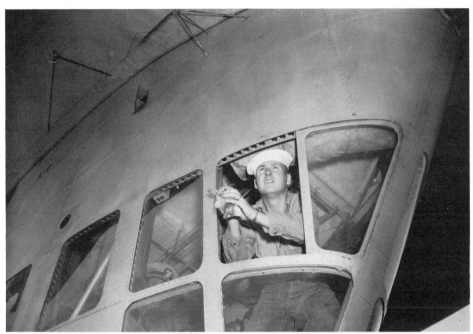

cock in May and June, respectively, the offshore waters of the Gulf of Mexico were essentially barren of the enemy, in sharp contrast to the year before. In mid-1942 German submarines had made the waters off the Louisiana coast a disaster area.

These Gulf-based squadrons kept trying, however, often in the face of extreme thunderstorm activity. ZP-23's pilots routinely attended the port director's meeting at Galveston prior to the departure of convoys. After briefings on convoy composition, course, speed, departure times, and the like by the port director, the convoy commodore, and the senior escort commander, pilots and ZP-23's ACI officer would meet with officers from the escort vessels and discuss how best to work together.

Moving his submarines about to take advantage of Allied defensive weaknesses and of target opportunities was Dönitz's style. One for exercising direct control over his forces, he or his chief of operations, Capt., later Rear Adm., Eberhard Godt, personally decided on the disposition of the U-boats, received their radioed reports, and sent them their radioed orders. This is how Dönitz masterminded and assembled the "wolf packs" for their massive attacks against convoys in the mid-Atlantic. After 30 January 1943, when he succeeded Grand Admiral Erich Raeder as Commander-in-Chief of the German navy, Dönitz could no longer give his U-boats the time and attention he had previously. He still kept his hand in, however, and whether Dönitz was present or not, Godt and others followed his strategic and tactical philosophies at the frugally staffed U-boat Command.*

One of the phenomena of the Battle of the Atlantic was the affinity that developed between merchant seamen and airshipmen. Merchant sailor after merchant sailor said the same thing: the sight of a blimp in company with his ship was reassuring, more so than that of a destroyer, corvette, or other surface escort, more so than that of an airplane.

The men of the merchant marine felt this way because they knew that, like their own vessels, surface escorts were vulnerable to underwater attack. The blimp was not. Airplanes, of course, were

---

* U-Boat Command was the operational side of Dönitz's submarine organization. Adm. Hans-Georg von Friedeburg, headed the administrative side seeing to personnel, training, logistics, and other support needs.

Proceeding with a convoy. (U.S. Navy)

not vulnerable either, but they came and went in a hurry and could not stay long. The blimp stayed with the convoy, flying low and throttling back to keep a slow pace. To the men on the freighters and tankers, the protection provided by an airship was a personalized thing. Airship crews and merchant ship crews waved to each other, the airship looking all the while majestic and overwhelmingly powerful and reassuring as it threaded its way through a convoy or kept station abreast or ahead of it.

The men in the blimps reciprocated this feeling of camaraderie. The same merchant ships plying the same coastal routes became familiar sights. Pilots found themselves in the role of mother hens, watching over the welfare of their charges in the water below. A surface vessel in difficulty was for them a matter of personal concern. Often a pilot or crew would take a special liking to a certain ship.

Lt. Comdr. James H. Cruse, for example, while flying with ZP-15, was fascinated by a brand new tanker he was assigned to escort. "That was one beautiful vessel," he recalled later,

> freshly painted, clean, and confidently plowing her way along on what well might have been her maiden voyage. I couldn't help but

admire her and I was determined no German was going to get this prize vessel while I was around. I flew coverage for her all day but at nightfall I had to return to Glynco. I radioed to request that another airship relieve me to stay with her through the night. The squadron was unable to send one. I thought about what might happen when she neared Hatteras and, no longer able to hug the shore, would have to go farther out to sea. Visibility was absolutely superb, about the best I could remember it having been. If there were Germans around, I thought they couldn't help but spot her.

I delayed my departure as long as I could, staying around until after dark so I could check her for lights and make sure she was blacked out. I came down low to the water, circled her, and could see no lights. I left but I was worried. That ship was such a splendid target for the enemy and I had begun to think of her as "my ship." The next morning at the Squadron Operations Office I looked at the board. Listed was "my ship," call letters KOZT, with the word SUNK next to it. I was shocked. I felt I had lost a friend.

Airships made nineteen antisubmarine attacks in 1943. On 3 March ZP-51's Trinidad-based *K-17* came upon and investigated an oil slick accompanied by air bubbles at 11°10'N, 061°50'W. The location was twelve miles from where other forces had delivered a night attack eleven hours previously. The target produced MAD signals, a dozen of them, and appeared to be moving slowly while the size of the slick increased. The *K-17* dropped three bombs with fifty-foot settings in a triangular pattern 150 yards ahead of it, producing an increase in the flow of oil. After the attack, further MAD contacts showed the object stationary. According to postwar information, there was no U-boat sunk there at that time.

On 26 March the *K-24*, also from ZP-51, was operating out of Guantanamo Bay. Its mission was to provide daylight escort of an inbound convoy and to cover a rendezvous point for about fifty ships five miles from the bay. Suddenly, it had an MAD contact in deep water. Coming about, it retraced its track, got another strong MAD signal, and alerted the area over the scene-of-action frequency. Within the next three or four minutes it recorded two more strong magnetic contacts two hundred yards southeast of the first. A PC boat reported a sound contact and dropped depth charges with no apparent results. The airship stayed on the scene but had no more contacts and released no bombs.

A month later, on 26 April, ZP-15's *K-45* dropped three Mark 17s with fifty-foot settings on one of several MAD contacts where no wreck was believed to exist. Owing to the shallowness of the water, about forty-two feet, only one bomb detonated. While the airship was flying a circular pattern, trying to search out where the U-boat might have gone, its radar scope suddenly showed a return astern. Looking aft, crew members saw a conning tower emerge on an estimated course of 225 degrees true and a bearing from the blimp of 150 degrees relative. The submarine, visible for about two minutes, was awash. It looked to have two periscopes. No deck gun could be seen.

The moment the submarine was sighted, the *K-45* was busy photographing an area of disturbed water containing elliptical sand streaks a quarter of a mile long and three hundred yards apart. Heading back immediately, the airship resumed its MAD search where the target had been seen to submerge and disappear. The needle of the MAD recorder swung five times on five different passes. With no bombs remaining on board, the *K-45* could only look for further signs that a U-boat was at hand. It observed two oil slicks, oval in shape, a quarter of a mile long, containing oily waste and fragments of wood. After seven hours surface craft arrived and relieved the *K-45*, which returned to base. According to operating doctrine, the pilot of an airship was the senior officer present afloat (SOPA) until relieved by the commander of a surface unit.

The *K-45's* radar contact, corroborated by its visual sighting, made it one of the most interesting airship incidents of the war but, because the blimp had no bombs remaining with which to attack, not very important. The shallow water did not necessarily preclude the presence of a U-boat. A Type VIIC's hull had a sixteen-foot draft. The height of the conning tower was about twenty feet. U-boat commanders were known to have found themselves occasionally in coastal waters shallow enough to threaten to ground them. Perhaps this had been the reason the submarine had surfaced. Besides, how to explain those sand streaks? Were they natural? Or had they been kicked up by a submarine's twin screws?

With radar, airships began to encounter disappearing nighttime "blips," an almost certain sign that the target had been a surfaced U-boat that submerged when approached. ZP-21's *K-40* picked up

71

A preflight briefing. (U.S. Navy)

one on 14 May.* The *K-53*, of the same squadron, detected another on 18 June. That blip was sharp and bright as it showed up on the port quarter of a line of ships, six miles from the closest of them and six miles from the blimp. It was a bright night with a full moon and scattered clouds. The K-ship must have been clearly visible as its turned toward and made for its target. At a range of about a mile, the radar return, which had been on the scope for a good five minutes, disappeared. The blips representing the convoy and its escorts remained unchanged. The presence of the airship had very likely kept the convoy from being attacked.

The ACI officers assigned to the squadrons briefed the pilots before departure. The ACI officers also interrogated them after they returned. It was the duty ACI officer's reponsibility to provide all the information needed for a mission. Assignments were received

* May 1943 was the turning point in the battle against the U-boat. Forty-one of them were lost during the month.

from sea frontier headquarters or from operational commands within the frontiers.

Because the Florida Straits were the U-boats' transit route between the Atlantic and the Gulf of Mexico and Caribbean, NAS Richmond was a busy place. It was home base to ZP-21, and airships on ferry flights between Lakehurst and the Caribbean and Brazil came through there. In addition, it was there that K-ships from the Gulf Coast, Caribbean, and Southern Hemisphere squadrons went for major overhauls.

All this flight activity considerably increased the workload of ZP-21's ACI officer, even though he had the help of his opposite number from the staff of Fleet Airship Wing Two. The wing, comprised of Blimp Squadrons Twenty-One, Twenty-Two, and Twenty-Three and of Blimp Headquarters Squadron Two, had first been commanded by Capt. Walter E. ("Heinz") Zimmerman, then by Capt. Maurice M. ("Mike") Bradley, both airship veterans who had seen service aboard the rigids, Zimmerman in the *Macon* and Bradley in the *Los Angeles*.

The ACI officers ran a round-the-clock operation out of Richmond's Hangar #3. They conducted their preflight briefings at the wing's offices in the station's administration building because aerology was located there and so were the telephones to the Gulf Sea Frontier headquarters in Miami. Postflight debriefings were done at the hangar to save tired pilots a trip across the station.

In addition to compiling a confidential flight folder containing information on the whereabouts of friendly submarines, estimated U-boat locations, radio frequencies and call signs, recognition signals, firing areas to be avoided, and shipping movements, the squadron ACI officer also prepared a track chart of the convoy or patrol areas to be covered. If two ZP-21 airships were assigned adjoining patrol areas, the chart specified the times at which they were to approach the common boundary. One would approach it on the even hours, the other on the odd. This arrangement would prevent collisions at night because if the two airships were to arrive at the patrol demarcation line at the same time, each would receive a radar return from the other and move in to investigate. Thus were pilots briefed and missions defined.

On the night of 18 July 1943 the pilot of ZP-21's *K-74*, although briefed that there were no U-boats in the area, encountered one on the surface and engaged it in a running gun battle unique in naval

Photography was important—of vessels escorted, craft and persons in distress, and, especially and always, evidence of any enemy presence. (U.S. Navy)

history. For years airshipmen and submariners had speculated about what would happen if blimp and U-boat ever met under such conditions. An answer was supplied that night in the Florida Straits.

The German participant in this unusual episode was the *U-134*, Kapitänleutnant Hans-Günther Brosin commanding. The *U-134* had not been a very successful war boat. In two years of service it had sunk only two ships.

The submarine was a Type VIIC with a crew of about forty-four who lived, as did all U-boat men at sea, in conditions unbelievable for their confinement, high humidity, and stench. It was 67.1 meters (about 220 feet) long, 6.2 meters (20 feet) across the beam, and 4.8 meters (16 feet) from the topside to the bottom of its hull. Seen today—the *U-995*, sole survivor of the type, can be visited at the German navy's memorial and museum at Laboe, near Kiel—a Type VIIC looks surprisingly small. Dönitz, although pressed by his

74

superiors to build large ones, wanted to keep his boats small so that they could maneuver readily, dive rapidly, and present the smallest possible sonar target. Type VIICs nominally carried fourteen torpedoes, which they launched from four torpedo tubes at the bow and one at the stern.

The *U-134* carried 113 tons of oil, enough for its twin 1,400-horsepower diesels to propel it on the surface for 8,500 nautical miles at ten knots or 10,000 nautical miles at seven knots. Maximum speed surfaced was about seventeen knots. Top speed submerged, using batteries and two 375-horsepower electric motors, was seven knots, a speed that it could not long sustain. More realistically, it could move underwater at four knots for eighty miles.

This was the enemy the *K-74* suddenly faced when, in ZP-21's Patrol Area One off Florida's southern tip, a bright spot appeared on its radar scope. Before being transmitted to base, contact reports from airships were encoded by referring to paper strips that substituted one set of letters or numbers for others. In the excitement of the moment, the *K-74*'s position was erroneously encoded as 23°59′N, 080°11′W. The mistake went unnoticed, so no correction was sent. The actual position was probably 23°59′N, 080°49′W.

The time was 2340. Flight altitude was five hundred feet, ground speed was forty-seven knots, and the target's range was eight miles.

Airship squadrons had by this time adopted the combat aircrew system in which the same ten officers and men flew together as a team. Each crew, however, would not fly the same airship for every mission, one of the reasons blimps were not more frequently named. The crew aboard the *K-74* that July evening consisted of Lt. Nelson G. Grills, command pilot; Ens. Darnley Eversley, navigator; Aviation Pilot Jandrowitz, copilot; Aviation Machinist's Mate 2nd Class Isadore Stessel, assistant mechanic; Aviation Machinist's Mate 3rd Class Schmidt, mechanic; Aviation Ordnanceman 3rd Class Eckert, rigger; Aviation Radioman 3rd Class Bourne, radio operator; Aviation Radioman 3rd Class Gidding, assistant radio operator; Aviation Radioman 3rd Class Rice, assistant radio operator; and Seaman 1st Kowalski, assistant rigger.

Visibility was better than twenty miles with ceiling unlimited. There was a three-tenths cloud cover of cumulus. The wind blew out of the southeast at ten knots. The surface tossed with moderate swells. A bright, almost full moon hung in the sky.

Grills alerted Richmond but was not at all certain his target was a submarine. Ordering battle stations, he headed for the source of the blip. Eversley was on the elevators, Jandrowitz was on the rudders, and Grills was standing behind them, conning the airship. Eckert, who had been a gunnery instructor, was in the machine-gun turret, and Stessel, who said he knew how to work the bomb releases, was at the bombardier's station.

As the blimp bore down on its radar target, a submarine was spotted silhouetted against the moonlit water. Everyone saw it. An after deck gun separate from the conning tower—after deck cannons were not normally carried by Type VIIC U-boats—was clearly visible. No one saw any deck gun forward. The *K-74* made a circle to the right to try to keep the submarine in view but lost sight of it anyway. The airship then flew another, wider circle and picked up the U-boat again by its wake.

According to doctrine, Grills was supposed to stay upwind and beyond the range of the enemy's guns while calling for air and surface support. He was to charge in and attack only if the U-boat started to dive or posed an immediate threat to shipping.

Grills knew very well what "the book" said. He knew, also, that Commodore Mills had been urging more aggresiveness on the part of pilots. There were merchant ships, a tanker and a freighter, about twenty miles distant. They were in no immediate danger, but the U-boat, running fast on the surface on a course of 220 degrees true, was headed right for them.

Doctrine be damned! At 2350 Grills started his bombing run.

For a while the *U-134* kept its course, showing no sign it even knew the blimp was there. The pounding of the submarine's diesels undoubtedly masked the droning of the approaching airship. But in the bright moonlight the German captain and his bridge watch could not help seeing the silver shape, probably well before the *K-74* had seen the submarine.

Grills drove ahead ... height 250 feet ... 1,700 RPM ... ground speed fifty-three knots ... target angle thirty degrees.

Suddenly, the *U-134* turned sharply to port to present its stern to the oncoming blimp. From about 250 yards it opened fire with the two 20-mm guns located on the *Wintergarten*, the railed platform at the aft end of the conning tower. The shooting from the conning tower stopped for five or ten seconds and then resumed.

As the airship came nearer, a bright flash and loud report signaled that the 88-mm had gone into action. This was followed by another boom in about twenty seconds, just after the *K-74* had overflown the submarine. Then by a third, ten or so seconds later. After that the cannon fire stopped. It had had no apparent effect. Later, when he was in the water, Grills noticed a hole a foot in diameter between the nose battens, an indication that at least one of the projectiles must have gone through the airship's bag without exploding.

With the hull of the *U-134* coming up fast, Grills altered course to cross it at a fifteen-degree angle so that the bombs would straddle the boat. Stessel pulled up on the releases to let go the two Mark 17s on the outboard racks. They were set to explode at fifty feet.

The bombs hung up!

At fifty-plus knots of ground speed, Grills was quickly past Brosin, who was firing away with his 20-mms. German bullets bracketed the car, thudding into the bag on either side. No hits were scored on the car itself except for a single hole in the Plexiglas of the gun turret. With his .50-caliber Browning, Eckert had gotten off sixty rounds, reloaded in the dark, and fired forty more. He had to stop when he could no longer depress the gun enough to hit the submarine. No one on the *K-74* could make out any enemy personnel on the conning tower or deck.

Hit, the *K-74*'s starboard engine burst into flames. They were quickly put out by its fire-extinguishing system. The port engine, probably also hit, fell off in RPM but picked up when Eversley advanced the throttle.

The crippled airship, flying in a steep nose-up attitude from having lost helium out of its shot-up stern, began falling. At 2355, with the propeller of its starboard engine windmilling and its port engine running, the airship entered the water, its nose pointing east. Dumping gasoline and dropping the slip tanks had done little to keep it in the air. With the bag limp, leaking, and deformed, there was no buoyancy or control.

"Everybody out!"

Grills made sure the classified folder was thrown overboard, taking care of that himself. Someone else tossed out the life raft, but without a line attached. It inflated and promptly drifted or blew away. The ten men left the airship through the windows, the main door on the starboard side aft, and the emergency door also on the starboard side just forward of the radioman's station.

The *K-74* would float for eight hours. Grills, seeing that it was not about to go under, went back aboard for a last look around, entering it through the elevatorman's window. He found the car deck completely covered with water. Aft of the mechanic's panel, everything was submerged. Sensing the car settling, he left, going out the way he came in and swimming around to the starboard side, where he expected to join his crew. He could not find them.

It was an anxious group of nine that Grills was trying to locate. Dependent on their life vests to help them stay afloat, they were adrift, so they estimated, thirty miles from the Florida coast. Even worse, they had no idea what the U-boat was up to. The tail-down attitude of the *K-74* as it had settled in had cut off all visibility aft. Actually, Brosin had dived. The airship's crew didn't know that and were concerned that the enemy might be poking around the area. So they backed away from the wreck. Later in the night, four crew members returned to the airship to take advantage of its buoyancy to help keep themselves up. The others stayed away at what they considered a safe distance.

NAS Richmond first learned of the action through another of ZP-21's airship's, the *K-32*, which happened to pick up a series of "OFUs," a distress message unique to the squadron, that meant "Urgent, Fired On." Bourne, the *K-74*'s radio operator, had sent the signals on his own initiative. Another radioman, J. J. Turek, aboard the *K-32*, decided upon hearing these transmissions that they had to be coming from the *K-74* and, also on his own, relayed the information to Richmond. Had it not been for these two aircrewmen, there's no telling when or how ZP-21 would have learned what was happening. It received no word of the action from any other source, partly because only ZP-21's airships knew what the "OFUs" meant.

At 0745 a twin-engined Grumman JRF amphibian, with the squadron commander, Lt. Comdr. Alfred L. Cope, aboard, reached the scene. He found the *K-74* barely afloat, with only the tip of its stern above water. Nearby were a group of five and another of four survivors. The surface being too rough for a landing, the plane went off to buzz the destroyer *Dahlgren*, fifteen miles away, and lead her to them.

It was 0815 on 19 July 1943 when the *K-74* finally vanished from sight. From four hundred yards away its survivors, except for Grills, watched it go under and heard its bombs explode, proof that they had been armed.

Isadore Stessel was in the group of five when the plane came into view. With the others he had formed a ring to splash and kick to attract attention. After the Grumman Goose showed it had seen them and went off to get the *Dahlgren*, the survivors regrouped, having become somewhat separated. A shark's fin was suddenly seen making for Stessel, who was fifty to sixty feet from the others. The unfortunate crewman, a poor swimmer who needed to be helped, had swallowed seawater and was vomiting. Eversley saw the shark make its attack. Stessel went under, reappeared with blood over his face and shoulders, and then sank again. The four who remained—three had knives—arranged themselves back to back for protection and got out of the blood-stained area as fast as they could. They saw other sharks but were not attacked. Shortly afterward the *Dahlgren* picked them up.

Grills, unable to locate his crew and thinking they had taken off in the raft, struck out for the Florida Keys. He had swum an estimated six miles when, late the next afternoon, the *K-32*, a continuing player in the drama, sighted him, thanks to the alertness of crew member M. E. May, an aviation machinist's mate 3rd class. Surface help was summoned. The pilot of the *K-74* was picked up by the *SC 657*.

May, along with radiomen Bourne and Turek, would be commended for his role in the episode. He would be cited for "... extreme diligence while serving as an after lookout on the K-32 on 19 July 1943. You sighted Lieutenant Nelson G. Grills, USNR, who had been adrift in the sea for more than eighteen hours from a distance of about 4000 yards on the port quarter of the ship after the blimp had passed by him and he was passing astern. Conditions of the sea, sun, and the small size of the object made sighting most difficult. Your sighting was responsible for the rescue of Lieutenant Grills who was severely sunburned and near exhaustion."

After a few days in a naval hospital in Miami, Grills returned to Richmond, to his crew, and to squadron duty.

His adversary, Hans-Günther Brosin, fared better for a while. Immediately after the exchange of gunfire, he radioed U-Boat Command that he had shot down a U.S. Navy airship. He made no mention of casualties but did report damage to his quick-dive tanks by machine-gun fire.

What he did after that remains a mystery. Following the war, the U.S. Naval Institute received from a former U-boat crew member photographs purporting to show the *K-74*'s wreckage being examined alongside Brosin's boat. The mass of crumpled balloonlike material depicted in the pictures has never been positively identified. It looks too lightweight, more like barrage balloon than airship fabric, although it could have come from one of the *K-74*'s air ballonets, which were made of lighter material than the outer hull. The supplier of the pictures wrote that he had been on a submarine that had rendezvoused with the *U-134* and that Brosin had transferred the pictures.

Did Brosin return and inspect the downed airship? With a group of survivors hanging onto it and another group keeping it within sight, could he have done so unseen? And would he have taken the time to do it, knowing, as he must have, that the action would immediately attract all U.S. naval forces in the vicinity to the scene.

He sent no message that he would or did examine the *K-74*. Years later Admiral Dönitz was unable to tell the author whether Brosin had. Brosin and crew met their deaths on 24 August 1943 when Britain's Royal Air Force sank the *U-134* off Vigo, Spain, making it one of the 739 submarines lost by Germany during the Second World War.

There were those who thought Grills was a hero and those who thought he was not. Some said he should be given a medal—he was, the Distinguished Flying Cross, after the war—while others suggested a court-martial for his having ignored doctrine and gone ahead on his own.

From Fleet Airships, Atlantic came this official comment:

> ... doctrine called for the use of trailing tactics until the submarine began to submerge. An immediate attack was not indicated since no friendly shipping was in the immediate vicinity. Airships are not presently sufficiently armed normally to justify an attack on a surfaced submarine and should not attempt one unless the submarine is in a position to attack shipping or the discovery of the submarine in a position which permits attack as the enemy surfaces. By guiding a killer group to a U-boat, an airship is performing valuable service and is showing good team work as an individual member of the antisubmarine team.

A nagging question, of course, was why had the bombs failed to drop. The L21A bomb release was tricky. One first had to depress the knob at the end of the release handle, keep it depressed, and pull the handle back to a detent to arm the bombs. Then one pulled it, in a second step, all the way back to release the ordnance. The L21A release had a record of malfunctioning. Had it done so? Had Stessel worked it properly? He was dead, and no one could answer for him.

Commodore Mills awards the Purple Heart to Nelson Grills after his attack against the surfaced *U-134*. (U.S. Navy)

As a result of the *K-74*'s experience, the L21A was modified and made simpler. Later it would be replaced by electrical switches.

Nelson Grills was not court-martialed. Commodore Mills ordered him to his staff at Lakehurst to develop airship antisubmarine doctrine and tactics. No man was ever better qualified by experience for the job.

Excitement in airship commands over the *K-74* peaked and fell. Pilots and aircrews looked forward to their chance to have a go at a real-life U-boat as Grills had. For the remainder of the year, that opportunity never came, but a number of near opportunities did. On 22 July ZP-21's ever-present *K-32* sighted what appeared to be a periscope, a sighting evaluated as a "possible" by the Gulf Sea Frontier. On 16 August the *K-81* of ZP-14 had a disappearing nighttime radar contact near where a U-boat was plotted. In Brazil ZP-41's *K-84* held down a radar contact during a night patrol on the 14th of October. And on 23 November, 20 December, and 26 December the *K-19*, *K-53*, and *K-108*, respectively of Squadron Twenty-One all reported disappearing blips.

6. INCIDENTS

⟋⟍ FIFTY TIMES IN 1943 airships found planes that were downed, vessels that were disabled, and boats with survivors who were awaiting rescue. As many as fifty U-boat victims were sighted at a time, on that occasion by the *K-52* of ZP-51 on 2 July. Even the Coast Guard had to be rescued: a blimp from Weeksville spotted thirty-six of the crew members of the cutter *Wilcox* the day after the vessel foundered.

On 11 October it was an airship crew's turn to be saved. Without warning the *K-66* (ZP-15) lost its upper fin, which fell over to port, leaving a large hole in the bag. One or more of the fin brace wire patches holding it to the envelope had failed, an unpleasant surprise. The *K-66* fell into the water. Fortunately, it was on a training exercise with an American submarine, which was on hand to rescue the crew. The blimp sank while it was being towed to shore. There were no casualties. The incident gave fortunate early warning of a widespread and dangerous condition because when the topside patches on other airships were inspected, they were found to be rotting. The problem was limited to K-ships operating south of North Carolina, in the Gulf, and in the Caribbean. Ultraviolet radiation in semitropical and tropical areas oxidized the sulfur in the rubber. Rain that fell on the envelope created a weak form of sulfuric acid, which collected in the patches and grew stronger the longer the process continued. Goodyear went to work right away to develop a substitute patch. Identifiable by a red mark, the new patches were shipped to the headquarters squadrons to replace the old. Airships needing patch replacement, meanwhile, were limited to airspeeds below fifty knots, and their rudder throw was restricted.

As flying hours increased, pilots developed more and more confidence in the K-ship and its ability to master the weather, including thunderstorms! Blimps, owing to their slow speed, were often unable to bypass or dodge these disturbances. In such cases, pilots had no choice but to go through them.

To do so one:

Put the ship in near equilibrium, neither "heavy" nor "light," but with a slight edge toward heaviness to help the blimp stay down while riding updrafts.

Trimmed the ship so that it entered the storm straight and level.

Had crew members stand by the toggles controlling the air dampers and air and gas valves.

Powered up the Homelite blower so air could be fed into the ballonets, or even into the helium chamber, to keep up the pressure.

Reeled in the trailing radio antenna.

Looked for a light spot in the cloud or frontal line.

Entered the light spot no lower than two hundred feet and no higher than four hundred feet (over water).

Penetrated the cloud at fifty knots, reserving maximum power for maneuvering.

Anticipated a rapid and violent updraft, countering it by keeping the bow down.

Flew blind while in the worst of the storm, trusting on the instrument readings and not on personal sensations.

Rode out the vertical currents, using the engines and dropping, as ballast, bombs and slip tanks to keep control and stay in the air.

Prepared for torrential rain and hail, also for blinding flashes of lightning.

Made ready for the down gusts that would be encountered when exiting the storm.

Throughout, kept constant watch on the pressure. If it went too high, it could split the envelope. Too low, it could cause it to wrinkle and fold, making the control lines go slack.

Such was the textbook procedure for taking a blimp through a thunderstorm. Here is how ZP-23's Lt. (jg) Earl W. Geyer described what it was actually like aboard the *K-77* on 6 November 1943:

We were to pick up a mission at 1600. Upon our arrival, it appeared as though a thunderstorm of moderate size was approaching the city of Galveston from the southwest. Nothing much out of the ordinary, we thought, as it did not appear violent.

As we proceeded with our job seaward, the wind increased. We actually fell behind the vessels we were escorting. The thunderstorm had now grown quite large. Lightning was more frequent and it did look threatening.

At 1840, the end of evening twilight, we left our mission. In the meantime, the storm had grown to a staggering size. It seemed almost unbelievable that one could grow so fast. We knew that we were in for it. Our radar gave us some idea of what we were up against and the extent of the area it covered. It appeared oval in shape, about 150 miles long and 50 miles wide.

I looked seaward for an avenue of escape, but clouds appeared from nowhere to cut off our retreat in that direction. Anyway the wind was too strong for us to make much headway toward the open sea. The radar showed us to be approximately twenty-five miles south of Galveston Island. Having a strong southerly wind, I decided to make shore the best we could. However the storm was upon us with rain and lightning almost at the start.

I informed my crew to make all arrangements for a possible abandon ship and to prepare for a hard rough ride. We were making good about seventy knots ground speed when, without warning, a seemingly invisible hand picked us up and tossed us skyward. At 1000 feet the ship plunged toward the sea, reversing course from north to due south despite all efforts to hold it to a northerly heading. Apparently the storm had reached such intensity that the air currents were beginning to throw us about at will. Both airscoops were opened but our descent occurred with such rapidity that at times our air and gas pressure fell to half an inch.

After getting back on course, we were again caught in the fury. Rain pounded against the Plexiglas with such force that the noise of the engines was drowned out. There was no let-up in our tossing and pitching. We tried to maintain an altitude of eight hundred feet, but a down-draft caught us and with another reversal of course we fell from 1000 to 40 feet. I ordered Ensign Woodward to throttle the engines back at this point to keep us from going down. Luckily this action checked our fall. We followed this procedure for both ascents and descents and found it very satisfactory. Several times gas and air pressure rose to three inches.

We finally saw a light amidst the blinding flashes of lightning and found it to be the Galveston Harbor entrance. We tried to flash a message to Harbor Entrance Control but were so obliterated by rain, lightning, and clouds that we doubted it was received. This was the last light or recognized landmark we would see for some time. Lightning was becoming so bad we had to wear dark glasses. At times we could see bolts of lightning apparently almost within arm's length. The car was illuminated by a bright bluish hue.

After leaving the Port Entrance of Galveston, we changed our course to almost due west. Every minute we had to fight using our engines to control ourselves in the up- and down-currents which tossed us at will. We tried to keep above 500 feet and below 1000, not knowing for sure whether we were over the city of Galveston or not. Radio beams and communications were impossible to use.

It was about 2020 when we sighted lights below and clearing skies ahead and finally got a bearing. Apparently, after leaving Galveston, we had passed into the center of the storm and were carried along its path, gradually working to the northern extremity.

In spite of strong southwesterly winds of forty knots, we arrived at NAS Hitchcock to find the base blacked out and water logged.

Geyer and his crew's experience was not unique. The airships of ZP-21 frequently faced stagnant or slow-moving weather fronts along the Florida coast. Many, in order to patrol their assigned areas properly, had to penetrate these fronts and their thunderstorms three or four times in a single flight. One pilot in ZP-21 was forced to fly eighty miles parallel to a front before he could find a likely spot to go through it. Another was tossed up and down between 100 and 1,200 feet and spun about in three complete circles, one after another, to the accompaniment of heavy rain and awesome lightning. Still another was blown so low that his bottom fin entered the water and, fortunately, lifted out again.

Commander Blimp Squadron Twenty-One was rightly proud when he wrote in November 1943, "Flying has not been discontinued even once on account of weather when a job has been assigned . . . the pilots doing this night work (and all of them get a chance at it) are a serious-minded group with a lot of guts."

This kind of flying resulted in a special dependence upon the forecasting skills of the base aerologist. At Glynco a new one reported aboard and proceeded confidently to make his first prognosis. Even though a cold front would be moving through, his prediction was for average flight conditions and no rain. He then announced that he would like to make his first flight in a blimp; he was put aboard one scheduled for a local, two-hour, radio-calibration check. That two-hour flight lasted eighteen hours! The frontal passage was horrendous. The airship was the *K-66*, before it lost its upper fin. It was forced to divert to NAS Jacksonville for emergency refueling and then to ZP-21's detachment at NAS Banana River (later the Patrick Air Force Base and Cape Kennedy area) for a second refueling. The weatherman, chastened by his experience, would be a long time regaining face.

In addition to thunderstorms, there was the hazard of icing. It proved in practice more psychological than real. According to navy findings, no airships were lost to in-flight icing during the war years. In supercooled clouds, ice formed on them only on the forward edges of small protuberances and wires, presenting no serious problem. Rime or nonglaze ice would not accumulate significantly on the envelope because, according to the National Advisory Committee for Aeronautics, the small droplets of supercooled clouds did not impinge on it in sufficient amounts, being deflected by the airship's low airspeed and the curvature of its bag. Missions, furthermore, were generally flown below five hundred feet, which was below the levels of most icing clouds. Glaze ice, formed by freezing rain and drizzle, was something else. A pilot running into that had quickly to look for clearer or warmer air, the latter being often found close to the ocean's surface.

The worst ice and snow problems were not those experienced in the air but at the mast. The added weight on the top of the envelope could buckle the landing gear and, in crosswinds, cause the airship to roll over on its side, crushing engine outriggers and fins.

Two K-ships of ZP-15, riding to masts at NAS Charleston, South Carolina, on the night of 15–16 December 1943 each collected an estimated nine thousand to ten thousand pounds of ice and snow. Two hundred navy men struggled all night to keep the ships upright and headed into the wind. Even the tried-and-true technique of pulling a line fore and aft across the top of the bag failed to break the ice loose. It was almost two inches thick. The airships and ground handlers were released safely from their ordeal when the air temperature rose.

Strong winds, of course, made ground handling difficult and dangerous. They also made ground speeds impossibly slow, nonexistent,

Ground handlers successfully struggle at NAS Charleston to save a snow- and ice-laden airship by keeping it "on its feet" at the mast the night of 15–16 December 1943. (U. S. Navy)

or even reversed. The ultimate in frustration must have been the time a group of men on horseback caught up with and passed by a blimp from ZP-23 that was battling headwinds over land. The horsemen then rode on ahead until they were out of sight.

As a result of headwinds, some airships had tight squeezes when returning to base. One blimp, belonging to ZP-14 at Weeksville, found it impossible to cover the last thirty-eight miles. After standing still for two hours with fuel running low, it diverted to NAS Charleston, making an emergency landing at the army's Camp Davis on the way. The army went all out to help. The airship landed to the presence of three hundred soldiers, three fire trucks, two ambulances, a crash truck, doctors, nurses, and a half-dozen asbestos-clad firemen.

Another squeaked by even more narrowly when it landed at its base with only eight gallons of gas remaining in its tanks.

The *K-68* did exhaust its fuel on 6 August 1943, but not owing to winds. It did so because it went to the assistance of navy planes engaging a surfaced U-boat (which later got away). The ZP-51 airship was on daytime patrol from Edinburgh Field, Trinidad, when it received the following message from base: "SUB ATTACKED 12-88, 64-15 X PROCEED VICINITY SEARCH FOR SURVIVORS WRECKAGE." The pilot, Lt. (jg) Wallace A. Wydeen, headed for that location straightaway while advising his air controller that he was low on gas. On the way, worried about his fuel, he had second thoughts and set a course for home.

Fifteen minutes later he heard, "SIGHTED SUB BEARING [garbled] X DROPPED DEPTH CHARGE X ON FIRE X ON FIRE X SEND HELP," over the scene-of-action frequency. At this, Wydeen changed course again to resume a heading for the scene. As he approached it, he could see an oblong object lying low in the water and down by the stern: the U-boat. A navy Lockheed PV-1 Ventura circled the blimp and radioed a warning against approaching too close owning to the submarine's antiaircraft fire. After twenty minutes of observing two Venturas attack the submarine, Wydeen, increasingly concerned about his gasoline, radioed that he could remain no longer. He was told to return to base. On the way home, he began to realize that he had exceeded his prudent limit of endurance and that he would have to make an emergency landing. He began looking for a place to set down, hoping to land with some fuel remaining and wanting no part of running completely dry and then having to select a landing spot. He was relieved, therefore, when after dark the *K-68*'s radar picked up a landmass he thought was Margarita Island.

Using the airship's spotlight, Wydeen looked for a likely landing place. Finding one, he dropped flares and put the *K-68* down on its wheel. The blimp rolled briefly, then stopped with its nose under a clump of scrub trees. The crew tied it down with the short and long handling lines and the drag rope. Wydeen radioed Edinburgh Field to say that he had landed on Margarita Island. To refuel the *K-68*, the army sent a plane from Trinidad to Margarita, but it found no airship there. A message from Wydeen subsequently revealed that he had actually landed on Blanquilla Island, a rocky and barren place that was home to about twenty Venezuelans. A ZP-51 airship, carrying tins of gasoline to lower to the *K-68*, was thereupon dispatched to Blanquilla. When it arrived there, it found the *K-68* deflated.

The airship had been tied to the trees overnight. Morning brought sunlight and warmth that expanded the helium and made the airship light and impatient to take to the air. To keep it on the ground, the crew loaded the car with rocks. Even so, as the winds increased to about ten or fifteen knots, the *K-68* began kiting and thrashing about, its car striking the trees. Three of the five lines holding it parted. Then it kited again, smashing into the trees and tearing holes in the forward part of the bag.

At this point Wydeen ordered the airship deflated. The forward rip panel was pulled, followed by the after one. The blimp, its gas and lift gone, settled to the ground, coming to rest on its port side. What had been a prancing steed moments before was now a lifeless expanse of aluminum-colored fabric, lying atop a gondola.

Squadron Fifty-One, having finally caught up with the *K-68*, began sending other airships to Blanquilla preparatory to salvaging the wreck. One of the first things they did was lower a line and haul up the blimp's classified folder and the security-sensitive parts of its radar and MAD.

The island was photographed from the air to determine how best to proceed with the salvage. Navy LTA had never engaged in this kind of operation before. The job fell to an ex-Goodyearite, Lt. Comdr. John B. Rieker, who was Commander Blimp Headquarters Squadron Five, the maintenance unit supporting Trinidad-based Fleet Airship Wing Five and its sole squadron, Fifty-One.

Rieker, another officer, and five enlisted men set foot on Blanquilla Island on 9 August from a small crash boat belonging to the army. They concluded that to do the salvage job they would need a shallow-draft vessel with powerful winches, also some lumber and a jeep. The vessel arrived the next day in the form of a navy net tender. To communicate with it, the *K-68*'s radio gear was removed and set up for business "outdoors."

The fins and car were pulled by winches through the surf onto the tender. The car was moved to the beach by rolling it on its landing wheel and pulling it by jeep. On the beach, it was placed on its side, put aboard two skiffs, and floated out to the tender. By 15 August the wreckage of the *K-68* had been evacuated.

For shepherding merchant ships in convoys, the navy's blimps, meanwhile, were proving versatile and valuable. Their ability to chase after errant vessels and bring them back into line created no-little demand for their services in policing maritime traffic. Some airships carried loudspeakers to help them in this task. Because communications were so important, particularly at rendezvous points, a signalman was occasionally carried along. One such rating had the experience of his life when, riding up forward in the cockpit, he was struck by a ship's mast.

The pilot, an ensign with 1,500 hours in K-ships, was making a message drop, trying to do the job of two by using the rudder pedals while at the same time manning the elevator wheel. Although using the pedals tended to disrupt a pilot's feel for his ship, its static condition, and its movement, this particular officer thought he could make a better approach if he worked the rudder pedals and elevator wheel himself. He had done so successfully on three prior drops.

This time was different. Approaching into the wind with both air dampers open and the starboard engine idling, he brought the nose over the stern of the merchantman at about a hundred feet. A gust shoved the blimp's bow to port. To compensate, he applied hard right rudder, revving the port engine to help swing the ship to starboard. The airship did not respond fast enough. The portside forward end of its car, below the machine-gun turret, collided with the surface ship's mainmast, which broke through the front of the car and snapped off twelve feet from its top.

Climbing to six hundred feet, the pilot checked the damage. The front window and the bombardier's window were gone. The bombardier's station had been crushed and shoved back. One of the storage boxes for the long lines was smashed.

Most serious was the condition of the signalman, who had been sitting in the bombardier's station. His right leg had taken the force of the impact. Bone protruded, and he was bleeding profusely, alternately losing and regaining consciousness. He was carried into the undamaged part of the car, where a tourniquet was applied to his leg and the bleeding stopped.

The airship was still flyable. Radioing for an ambulance, the pilot returned to base. But his problems were not yet over. Approaching the field, the copilot found that when he applied hard right rudder to line up with the runway, his controls jammed. Plexiglas had gotten into the linkage of the rudder steering column. So the pilot was forced to use his engines for lateral control, with the result that he came in too fast for the ground handlers. On his second and successful approach he made sure he had enough tension on his rudder cables by having one of the crewmen reach up inside the car, grab the cables, and pull out any slack.

As a result of this unusual accident, the pilot was congratulated for "extricating the blimp from its perilous position." At the same time, he was reprimanded by the squadron commander for getting himself into the fix in the first place.

Follow-on measures were taken. The length of message-drop lines was increased to at least one hundred feet, with twice the usual trailing weight; henceforth, rudder pedals were not to be used during drops; pilots were to be reminded of "the directional instability of K-type blimps and the necessity for continuous close rudder control"; and morphine would be carried in the airships' first-aid kits. The signalman recovered, his convalescence made more pleasant by the radio sent him by the airship crew he had come to know under such unforgettable circumstances.

Another incident resulted in the incredible spectacle of an airship's making its way down a seaplane ramp into a river and setting sail toward the sea. The place was Naval Air Station Charleston. The star of the show was ZP-15's *K-34*. The supporting players were Lt. Lawrence J. Mack, pilot; Lt. Comdr. Jack H. Nahigian, operations duty officer; and Fireman 3rd Class H. F. Mras the unwilling cause of it all.

At 0520 on 20 November 1943 the *K-34*, 2,100 pounds "heavy," with the usual crew of ten aboard, prepared to take off from runway 36. The ground crew held the lines as it was taken off the mast and the mast hauled away. After a final check the operations duty officer (ODO) began making a circular motion with each arm, the signal to rev up the engines and take off. The *K-34*, moving slowly at first, began to pick up speed and steering control. The ODO then signaled to the men on the lines to let go, as he himself ran to the side to get clear of the oncoming airship. As he did, he was alarmed to see that the starboard line had caught Mras, one of the handlers, around the legs. He had been knocked down and was being dragged along the ground. With shouts and hand signals, Nahigian ordered the takeoff aborted and the drag rope released.

When an airship burned, not much was left. This is what remained after the *K-102* caught fire while being refueled in Hangar #1 at Glynco on 6 August 1944. Other aircraft in the hangar were evacuated to safety. There were no injuries to personnel. (U. S. Navy)

Mack, also seeing the entangled sailor, cut the engines, reducing the speed of the blimp and making it impossible to steer. The airship came to the end of the runway and to the seaplane ramp. Its momentum took it down the ramp and into the Cooper River, with Mras still caught up in the line. When the *K-34* entered the water, the strain on the line relaxed, and Mras was able to free himself. Mack went to his assistance, ordering his copilot to take over and jumping out of the pilot's window.

The airship, in the meantime, was beginning to sail majestically downstream with its crew still on board. Crash boats arrived to take it in tow and return it to the ramp. The ODO boarded the blimp from one of the boats and dropped the bombs unarmed into the river, marking the spot with a yellow buoy anchored by a grapnel. The airship was pulled back up the ramp and onto the apron by its drag rope. From aborted takeoff to remasting, the episode had taken just over an hour. Surprisingly, the *K-34* had suffered little damage. The bombardier's window had been broken, and water had entered where he put his feet. The main deck of the car had remained dry. The radar hat was crushed.

Nahigian had saved the ship by directing its recovery from the water. Mack had saved Mras. When he dived into the water to help him, he found a dazed line-handler who was being swept downriver. He helped the struggling sailor to safety aboard a seaplane mooring buoy. Mras would almost certainly have died had it not been for Mack. Some weeks later Mack would be awarded the Navy and Marine Corps Medal "for heroic conduct in saving the life of H. F. Mras, F3C." A citation from the president of the United States accompanied the medal.

Two other incidents in 1943 resulted in medals: one for making the first "on the wheel" rescue, the other for "bringing back alive" a K-ship that had crashed into the water.

The *K-65*, piloted by Lt. Comdr. Louis M. Ayers, was dispatched on 21 September with two other airships from ZP-21 to search for a missing British A-30 Baltimore bomber. When a navy plane found the bomber, the *K-65* and *K-70* were ordered to the spot. While the *K-70* stood by, Ayers decided to attempt a rescue, the first time in the war that an Atlantic Fleet airship set down in an inaccessible area to pick up survivors unassisted.

The A-30 had landed wheels-down in an open area on Andros Island in the Bahamas. At the end of two deep wheel tracks, 250 feet long, the plane lay on its back. Flying only a few feet above the ground, Ayers followed footprints that led from the wreck to a clump of trees. There he found two crew members. He shouted down to them that he was planning to land and pick them up. After a couple of practice passes, he approached the two men, putting the *K-65* on the wheel at the edge of the water and using the resistance of the water to slow it down. The stranded men grabbed the short lines, and the blimp came to a stop. Then the survivors dropped the ropes and rushed around to the starboard side to climb aboard. Ayers took off and delivered them to an improvised ground party of Royal Air Force men at Main Field, Nassau.

"Lou" Ayers would be awarded the Air Medal for this recovery. It was a type of rescue that would be repeated a number of times in

Ground crews literally gave their shirts when it came to plugging helium leaks like this hole in the *K-46* at NAS Richmond. (U. S. Navy)

jungle clearings, in mainland and island areas, on sandy beaches—indeed, wherever a low, flat, slow approach to survivors could be made. Often these rescue-landings followed preliminary runs to test the firmness of the landing surface and to drop off a crew member who would instruct the survivors about how to handle the lines and board the airship. In time, landing on the wheel to pick up stranded persons would become commonplace. It was Ayers who accomplished it first and showed it could be done.

A crash on 30 October brought to Lt. Comdr. Alfred L. Cope, the commander of ZP-21, the Distinguished Flying Cross for flying one of his squadron's airships out of the drink and getting it back to base. The incident began at 0556 when the *K-17*, on a ferry flight from NAS Richmond to NAS Lakehurst, was flown into lower Biscayne Bay by an inattentive ensign pilot who admitted to having had only two hours of sleep the night before.

95

The impact, taken bow-down, threw the rudder operator into the machine gunner's turret, where he received minor head injuries. The radar operator was thrown, uninjured, out the window. All of the windows were broken. The lower half of the car was under water. The port propeller was badly bent. The radio was knocked out. By blinker and with red flares the crew attempted to attract attention and get help. A navy seaplane, a Chance Vought OS2U, responded by landing alongside, picking up the injured man, and taking him to the Dinner Key Coast Guard station.

As the sun rose, the helium warmed and superheat developed. Helium had to be valved to keep the *K-17*, growing ever lighter,

It was a pitiful sight when an airship struck the side of a hangar while docking or undocking. Here, heroic measures are in process at Richmond to save the *K-86*. (U. S. Navy)

On 21 September 1943 in the *K-65* "Lou" Ayers made the first wheel-landing rescue when he picked up two fliers from this crashed A-30 on Andros Island in the Bahamas. (U. S. Navy)

from lifting itself off the water. Cope arrived in a crash boat at 0843. Deciding to try to fly the airship back to Richmond, he ordered slip tanks, chairs, and equipment removed to lighten the weight. Then he started the starboard Pratt and Whitney and took off at 0915. Thirty minutes later one beat-up K-ship landed safely at its home base.

7. TROPICAL CLIMES

IN JANUARY 1942, as a follow on to *Paukenschlag*, Dönitz sent boats to the Caribbean to attack shipping off Aruba, Curaçao, and Trinidad. In the absence of effective antisubmarine measures in that area, these U-boats and those that followed them enjoyed tremendous success. Beginning in April, tanker submarines helped the U-boats operate so far from home. These so-called "milch cows," the large Type XIV, displaced 1,932 tons submerged and carried more than 400 tons of diesel fuel for resupplying other U-boats.

Action in the Caribbean had subsided by the time the *K-17*, the first of ZP-51's airships to fly out of Trinidad, arrived on 16 February 1943. It operated from a U.S. Army facility at Edinburgh Field, where there were two airplane runways in addition to mooring circles built for LTA use. Edinburgh, later named Carlsen Field for an army officer, became the home of Blimp Squadron Fifty-One, Blimp Headquarters Squadron Five, and Fleet Airship Wing Five. Their operating area extended from Trinidad as far south as Brazil.

The changes in command at Trinidad reflected the game of musical chairs under way as the Atlantic Fleet airship organization expanded. Command of ZP-51 was held sequentially by Zurmuehlen, Reppy, Bailey (all previously mentioned), and Lt. Comdr. Robert J. Williams within an eight-month period; command of Blimp Headquarters Squadron Five by Rieker, Lt. Comdr. John D. Lautaret, and Lt. D. R. Grace within six months. Reppy had become the wing commander on 2 August 1943, when he also became the commanding officer of ZP-51. He would be relieved by Bailey on 6 October when the latter assumed the wing and squadron command.

Back in Washington, D.C., navy planners were preparing for the construction of one of the thousand-foot-long wood and concrete hangars at Edinburgh Field. The airshipmen on site said they had

Carlsen, also known as Edinburgh, Field, Trinidad, British West Indies. (U.S. Navy)

no need for it. Meanwhile, a navy construction battalion showed up to start building when the materials arrived. Eventually, a compromise was reached. A small steel-frame hangar was erected that had once housed army blimps in the States. It was big enough to hold one K-ship.

Capt. Thomas G. W. "Tex" Settle and Chief Boatswain Frederick J. Tobin had surveyed Caribbean sites for LTA bases. They must have looked an incongruous pair, Settle short and thin, Tobin large and bull-chested. Tobin, the popular image of an old-time navy chief, had been an aviation chief rigger on rigid airships.

Settle, a "can doer" who had graduated second in his class at the Naval Academy in 1917, had been communications officer aboard the *Shenandoah* and engineering officer aboard the *Los Angeles*. As inspector of naval aircraft at Goodyear-Zeppelin, he had overseen the building of the *Akron* and *Macon*. His long-distance flights in national and international ballooning competitions had made him the "winningest" balloon racer in the navy. In 1933 he had set a supreme world's altitude record of 61,237 feet in a stratospheric balloon, becoming the first American to pilot a pressurized cabin into the upper air. He was the only person in the history of flight qualified to pilot an airplane, a glider, a free balloon, and a blimp and to command a rigid airship. His achievements were legendary in LTA.

Tobin was no less legendary. He had survived the wreck of the *Shenandoah* in 1925 and had flown the *Los Angeles* so often as elevatorman and helmsman that he was considered part of the ship. He typified the leading chief, always available when needed and always knowing what to do. His dependability had never been more evident than when the *Hindenburg* burned at Lakehurst. Tobin was in charge of part of the ground crew at the time the German Zeppelin burst into flames and began falling. The men broke and ran, but the bellowing voice of "Bull" Tobin stopped them in their tracks: "NAVY MEN, STAND FAST! THERE ARE PEOPLE IN THERE AND WE'VE GOT TO GET THEM OUT! STAND FAST!" They did and, led by Tobin and other chiefs, entered the blazing wreckage to bring out survivors. Sixty-two people were saved out of the ninety-seven on board. Many owed their lives to Tobin and to the other navy men who risked their own that evening. Later, in May 1943, Tobin was commissioned a lieutenant.

The commandant of Naval Operating Base Trinidad was the local operational commander of forces in that sector of the Caribbean Sea Frontier. He assigned ZP-51 its missions to be flown from Edinburgh Field and, by the squadron's detachments, from Atkinson Field, British Guiana, and Paramaribo, Dutch Guiana. It was fortunate that he was the one who did. The commander of the Caribbean Sea Frontier, Rear Adm. John H. Hoover, was not supportive of blimps, pretty much ignoring them even though they were assigned to his command. He ran a decentralized sea frontier, with the commandants at Trinidad, Guantanamo, and Curaçao calling their own operational shots. Fortunately for airship operations in the Caribbean, the commandant of the naval operating base at Trinidad was of a different mind from Hoover. Airship operations in the area were well coordinated with his headquarters. To ensure that they were, Lieutenant Commander Cruse, formerly of ZP-15 and to whom a certain torpedoed tanker had meant so much (see chapter 5), was assigned to his staff.

Atkinson Field, home of ZP-51's British Guiana detachment, lay twenty-three miles south of Georgetown, a place of sixty-nine thousand people. It had been and would continue for some time to be a base for navy HTA. The blimp squadron detachment, mooring circles, and masts, plus a two thousand–foot northeast-southwest runway, were about a mile from the airplane activities. The detachment's operations office was located at Atkinson's navy air control center. Most of the missions assigned to the blimps at Atkinson, as at Edinburgh, were daytime patrols.

The Paramaribo detachment, located three miles southwest of that town of fifty-five thousand inhabitants, was apart from any other naval activity but adjacent to a U.S. Army camp. It had the usual airship gear and a two thousand–foot strip for takeoffs and landings. Day and night patrol missions were flown, centering about Paramaribo, the departure point for ships carrying bauxite from Dutch Guiana to Trinidad. The Lower Bauxite Run from Paramaribo to Georgetown was covered by Paramaribo-based airships, the Upper Bauxite Run by those at Atkinson. At Trinidad the bauxite was reloaded into large ore carriers for shipment north. Local roads in and around ZP-51's Paramaribo base, being built of materials containing this aluminum ore, were remembered by pilots as among the most valuable in the world. They also remembered the vampire bats that fed on local cattle.

Twenty-five miles from ZP-51's Paramaribo site, with its collection of single-story wooden structures with screened walls, was Zandery Field, where a navy HTA squadron of patrol bombers was based. At Paramaribo and at Zandery, assignments were received daily by dispatch from Naval Operating Base Trinidad, which also supplied U-boat estimates and other operational intelligence.

ZP-51 had yet another detachment, one at NAS San Juan, Puerto Rico, which served as a refueling stop for airships ferried between Richmond, Florida, and Trinidad. On those flights pilots sometimes dosed themselves with benzedrine sulfate to ward off fatigue. A senior pilot, well known for his competence and professionalism, aptly demonstrated the side effects when he landed there under its influence. The ship had been masted when the ground-crew chief came aboard and asked, "Any special instructions, Commander?"

101

"No, Chief, just put the ship in the hangar."

"But Commander . . ."

"Chief, don't argue with me. Put the ship in the hangar!"

What the chief was trying to say was that San Juan had no airship hangar.

The third Guiana, farther south than those of the British and Dutch, belonged to the German-controlled French government. Landings and overflights were not permitted there. From offshore, pilots and aircrews could sometimes see the lights of Devil's Island.

Beyond the Guianas lay Brazil, the operating domain of Blimp Squadrons Forty-One and Forty-Two, Blimp Headquarters Squadron Four, and Fleet Airship Wing Four. All were part of the Fourth Fleet, which was headquartered in Recife. The wing commander, Captain Zimmerman, had his offices downtown in the same "navy building."

ZP-41's airships began arriving in Brazil in the fall of 1943. The *K-84*, first of the squadron ships, left Lakehurst on 10 September, setting down at Fortaleza, Brazil, on the 27th, after 4,430 nautical miles and 98 flying hours. It had made the longest navy airship ferry flight yet; had been the first nonrigid to cross the equator (the rigids *Graf Zeppelin* and *Hindenburg* had done it many times); and had landed in five different "countries": NAS Guantanamo Bay in Cuba, Edinburgh Field in Trinidad, Atkinson Field in British Guiana, Paramaribo in Dutch Guiana, and Amapa, Igarape Assu, and, finally, Fortaleza in Brazil.

Amapa, the northernmost ZP-41 base in Brazil, was on a prairie 133 feet above sea level, 12 miles in from the coast, at 02°06'N, 050°48'W. A former Pan American Airways field, it was host to the army's Air Transport Command (ATC) as well as to ZP-41. There was no other navy activity there. From the standpoint of flight operations and living conditions, it was a hardship base, especially during the rainy season from January to June.

If Amapa was bad, Igarape Assu—02°35'S, 044°15'W—was worse. Besides blimps, only small planes could use it.

The main base for ZP-41 would be only six miles away from São Luiz, which was a city of eighty-four thousand. The blimpron and blimphedron detachment would share Tirirical Airport with Pan American, the ATC, and navy HTA. Until São Luiz was ready, the squadron had its headquarters at Fortaleza.

Navy LTA and navy HTA, in the shape of two blimps, three PVs, and one PBY, share the field at São Luiz, Brazil. (U.S. Navy)

At Fortaleza blimps and navy patrol bombers operated from Pici Field. They were given pretty much of a free hand by the commander of the Fourth Fleet in deciding their own missions. Fourth Fleet headquarters was mainly a supplier of intelligence, informing the naval air units at Pici if there were U-boats plotted off the coast and advising of shipping to be protected. It was left to the local LTA and HTA commanding officers to decide what their K-ships and Lockheed Venturas would do. In the absence of U-boats or shipping, the time was spent in training.

Recife, as all liberty hounds were quick to note, was a city of 491 thousand. Its Ibura Field, nine miles southwest of town, was little used operationally, even though it had a mooring circle and mast. Recife's importance was as an administrative command center.

Ibura was not without its resident celebrity: an enormous black bird that was tied to a perch for all to admire. Nearby was a long pole to poke and prod the fierce-looking creature in expectation of

103

a great flurry of feathers and a blood-chilling screech or scream. It was great fun to watch visitors, stick in hand, gingerly approach the great bird, apprehensively give it a couple of pokes, and then beat a hasty retreat as it turned, glowered, and opened its mouth. All that came out was "PEEP"! Meeting the bird was one of the rituals of the base.

Before the war, Recife, meaning "reef" and correctly reflecting that part of the coast, had been a terminus for the *Graf Zeppelin* in its flights between Germany and Brazil. Jiquia, where it had landed and been moored, was about two miles from Ibura. The Brazilians had made the *Graf's* landing field into an ammunition dump.

Blimp Squadron Forty-Two, based still farther down the coast, south of the "bulge," had its main base twelve miles northwest of Maceió, a Brazilian city of 133 thousand. Navy HTA as well as LTA flew in and out. There was also a Pan American and Brazilian army presence.

LTA moved into Brazil to the accompaniment of two songs then enjoying great popularity in the United States. The one was "Brazil," as played by orchestra leader Xavier Cugat. The other was "Tico Tico," a catchy rhythmic tune, the beat of which represented the movement of the Tico Tico bird as it hopped about. ZP-41 and ZP-42 pilots hummed these melodies as they headed south toward Brazil, Rio de Janeiro, and Rio's Copacabana Beach. "The Girl from Ipanema" had not been heard of yet.

A far cry from the mosaic sidewalks, soft white sand, and powerful undertow of Rio's Copacabana Beach was the remote, barren, and rocky island of Fernando de Noronha. Three hundred miles off the Brazilian mainland and only seven square miles in size, it was a penal colony named for an early buccaneer. A great shaft of rock, a kind of poor man's version of Rio's Sugar Loaf, reached high into the sky, calling to mind that larger and much more famous geographical feature. On this remote island an airship mooring circle was laid out, a mast set up, and a detachment of one officer and forty-three men established. Regular operations from Fernando were not planned, the detachment being intended for backup or emergency use.

An inspection trip to the island brought a close call for Commodore Mills. Returning from Fernando to the mainland, the R50 carrying the Commander Fleet Airships, Atlantic and his staff had both engines sputter and go dead when it entered a localized area of

Flying down to Rio. (U.S. Navy)

unusually heavy rain. As it glided out of the downpour and back into sunshine, "Hal" Leedom, the pilot, was able to start the engines again. The situation saved, he was later heard to mutter something about how it was high time to get some pressurized ignition harnesses installed.

São Salvador, a city of 365 thousand people, was also known as Bahia. An unusual city built on two levels, it was thirteen miles from Ipitanga Field, which ZP-42, more navy PVs, Pan American, and Brazil's air force shared. Ipitanga was noted for the high sand dunes that surrounded it on all sides except to the east. A navy flying boat, a PBY Catalina, with one engine out, was making a forced landing in the area one dark and bumpy night when it grazed one of the dunes and slid to a halt, the pilot unaware that it had until a waist gunner, thrown out by the impact, walked up alongside and waved through the window at him. At least that was how the story went.

105

The next airship base to the south was Caravelas, also known as Malaria Manor. It was a grassy flying field originally used by Air France.

Then came Vitória, more a refueling site than anything else, with its scenic harbor that looked like a scaled-down version of Rio's.

And, finally, Rio de Janeiro.

In the mid-1930s the Brazilian government had erected a hangar 820 feet long and laid out a 1,000-acre landing field at Santa Cruz outside of what was then the capital, there being no Brasília at the time. This field was originally for the German commercial airships *Graf Zeppelin* and *Hindenburg*. Until ended by the latter's destruction at Lakehurst in 1937, theirs had been a highly successful and popular service, partly because it accommodated the sizable German community in Rio, partly because people traveling between Germany and Brazil by Zeppelin could make the trip in three and a half days, whereas the steamer took three weeks. President Getulio Vargas, aware of the value of the German airships for bringing trade and commerce to Brazil, had supported the German suggestion that his government build a facility to land and house the ships.

The hangar at Santa Cruz, its steel girders, wooden roof, and stucco-covered brick walls with long perpendicular rows of windows and longitudinal runs of skylights, was like the Zeppelin hangars recently built in Germany. When Blimp Headquarters Squadron Four arrived, commanded by Gerry Zurmuehlen, it found there the mobile mast used to haul the big ships in and out of the shed on railroad tracks, spare girderwork that had been kept on hand for making repairs, sandbags, gas-storage facilities, and some high-reach ladders. Elements of the Brazilian air force occupied the hangar and field.

The first navy blimp to use Santa Cruz was the *K-84*. Its arrival was described by Zurmuehlen in his Headquarters Squadron Four newsletter of 19 November 1943:

> Last week saw the first K-type airship docked in a South American hangar. The large city and its newspapers were boisterous in a welcome for the "simpatico bleemp" although there were numerous worried comments from the civilian population concerning the return of the Germans.* In line with the "good neighbor policy" and in

* Brazil, its patience exhausted by U-boat attacks on its shipping, had declared war against Germany in August 1942.

The hangar used by the German airships *Graf Zeppelin* and *Hindenburg* at Santa Cruz. (U.S. Navy)

compliance with a request from the Air Ministry, a flight was made over a holiday gathering attended by the President on the afternoon of its arrival.

No Navy personnel were as yet located at the refueling base [Vitória] north of the big town and transportation was available for one man only to arrive there ahead of the K-84. Somehow the HedRon Commander did and, in his best Portuguese, explained how to land, refuel, and prepare a blimp for takeoff to seventy-five laborers who are building quarters and a landing mat at that base. None of them could speak English and the HedRon Commander has a very limited command of Portuguese. At any rate, with many "*Afrouxar*'s" ["Slack off's"] and "*Puxar para tras*'es" ["Pull that way's"], and a few "*Vai embora*'s," the ship was handled, the crowd (?) kept back, and two small dogs shooed away. With a sore throat and perspiration from sheer relief, the HedRon Commander was assisted aboard by Pilot

107

Leftenant J. N. Rose and a lovely takeoff in the best Lakehurst-approved manner followed.

The flight down was uneventful, strong tail winds, and smooth flying until 2300 when fog set in. The land of granite-lined clouds is no place for night-fog cruising in any kind of aircraft, so, after definitely establishing position, the K-84 hove to on one engine awaiting daylight. At daylight over the top of the fog, the upper 200 feet of a famous landmark [the peak known as Corcovado, with its giant statue of Christ on top] could be seen and easily recognized. Soon after we passed it, a hole opened up and the town could be seen below. The rest of the trip was made inland through the pass and a safe landing made in the hands of Lt. Blair's ground crew. This ground crew, which had only five Qualified Lighter-than-Air ratings out of the 150 personnel on station, having seen Lt. Comdr. Becker and a blimp in a training film, knew what the K-84 was and accepted the situation. It was landed and docked. . . .

For the ground handling prior to the goodwill flight, the HedRon Commander successfully relieved Bos'n Desmond and by stretching memory (the last time associated with a hangar was 1940, or was it 1939?) managed to maneuver a mighty slow tractor to get it out and later back through a skinny door in a partial cross-wind. Lt. Blair piloted the ship for the flight and, in spite of fog, low ceiling, and questionable weather, gave the populace quite a thrill and greeting.

Zurmuehlen's account was intentionally a bit vague, making no specific reference to Brazil or to Rio by name. He was writing for his weekly newsletter, which was classified Restricted. The precise locations of the operating units of Fleet Airships, Atlantic were Confidential. To maintain security, they had Fleet Post Office addresses.

Blimp Headquarters Squadron Four had a special interest in the Santa Cruz hangar because inside it the airships of ZP-41 and ZP-42 would undergo major repairs and overhauls. The HedRon detachments in the field would do minor repairs, Santa Cruz performing those jobs beyond the capabilities of the detachments along the coast. The really big ones, like reerecting an airship that had been deflated, would be reserved in most cases for the assembly and repair department at NAS Lakehurst or NAS Richmond.

The scheduling of maintenance and overhauls varied during the war years as experience was gained. Generally, the blimps of Fleet Airships, Atlantic underwent major overhaul, that is to say tear down, rebuilding, and rebagging, every 3,840 flight hours. When the deleterious effect of the sun on southern-based ships was discovered, the time between major overhauls was changed. Blimps operating south of Weeksville were to have them every twelve months, north of Weeksville every eighteen.

In the tropics, it seemed, just about everything rotted except envelopes. A shipment of nose battens fell apart, the casein glue holding together their laminated spruce strips having become a victim of the heat, humidity, and bacteria. The fabric on the fins also gave way, at first at the leading edges of the elevator surfaces and then all over.

The envelopes stood up surprisingly well. Consider the case of reconditioned bag D386, which bore the *K-48*. "It has flown almost wholly in northern Brazil," said a HedRon Four newsletter.

> It has been flying from a mast in the wettest tropical area for one year. Six inches of rain fell on it within a twenty-four hour period and a mere noticeable washing away of the aluminum paint was observed the next day. The blue U.S. Navy lettering has almost faded away. It is amazing that an envelope survives as well as it does. Day after day it takes the worst weather possible. Such things as canvas cots, that get wet and then dry in the sun, rot and break almost immediately. Wood rots quickly. The process of corrosion is stepped up in everything.

In addition to the major overhauls, there were interim ones, usually every 960 hours. These were performed by the blimphedrons at Santa Cruz, Richmond, and Lakehurst and took about ten days. Every 120 hours, airships were given a check of engines and major systems. This was done on the mast. Engines were changed by using work stands and hoists.

Rio de Janeiro, the Paris of the Southern Hemisphere, was what every airshipman wanted to see. Famed for the beauty of its setting, as well as for the beauty of its beaches and its women, although not necessarily in that order, it was a magical place that offered exotic shopping and nightclubbing. Buying gemstones could be euphoric at the prices asked. So, too, the pairs of handmade leather shoes. It was a euphoria that all too often gave way to disillusionment when the true value of the emeralds was later discovered or when the footwear had its first encounter with rain. Safer bets were the wooden statuettes, the alligator-skin belts and pocketbooks, and the trays underlaid with pictures made of multicolored butterfly wings.

For evening entertainment there was the Urca nightclub, starring the sultry and beautiful movie star Ilona Massey. She really packed them in to hear her sing "Love for Sale." Miss Massey was a real trooper, volunteered to visit the airship bases, and got as far north as ZP-51–land. When her mode of transportation was blimp, her modesty was safeguarded by a curtain daintily hung in front of the head. At one of ZP-51's detachments, she wowed all hands to such an extent they went right out and painted "Lovely Ilona" on the car of the *K-100*. The only entertainer so honored by airshipmen during the war, she added her autograph under the freshly painted name.

For a specially sophisticated evening on the town, one went to the Copacabana Palace Hotel. There, in the superbly romantic Midnight Room, one was entranced by the rhythm and the spectacle of an authentic samba.

So that officers and men in the Brazilian boondocks could enjoy some of these pleasures, the hedron PBY flew leave and liberty parties to Rio.

Operations in Brazil with its steaming climate gave new importance to superheat and the problems of maintaining the gas purity of the ships. Zurmuehlen noted that, after six months of gadding about in that sultry clime, the *K-84* had become a "bottle addict," having consumed twenty-five bottles of helium at one location. He unfortunately lacked the equipment in the field to "purge" the airship, that is, recycle its gas to remove the air that had contaminated it. The less pure the helium, of course, the less the lift.

At the bases in Brazil, native help was used for ground handling and general work around the place. The locals were glad to be paid, but they were also very proud of their roles. Working at the base made a man a big shot in his village.

Native help was a mixed blessing. It was useful when needed, but it could also be light-fingered. At Amapa one night two workers went so far as to break into the BOQ (Bachelor Officers Quarters being a rather unnecessary name in view of the circumstances under which everyone was living). Discovered, they were chased into the wee hours until finally caught. It was at Amapa that one of the native helpers was brought in with a knife blade in his chest, the result of a local difference of opinion.

The detachment at Amapa was the scene of a continuing struggle between navy men and local fauna. For a while, so many semidomesticated cattle took to roaming about the field that ground-handling officers had to carry a shotgun in addition to the usual whistle and megaphone. If shouts and curses didn't move the cattle, a load of shot would. One night a large humpbacked bull, not liking the way his pasture was being lit up, charged the portable floodlight and demolished it.

The BOQ at Amapa was the locale of another encounter of a quite different kind. A group of pilots unexpectedly came face to face with a boa constrictor. Everyone, the snake included, took up a reciprocal heading.

Slithering creatures could be a problem in tropical climes. At Amapa a pilot retrieving a volleyball from the grass was bitten by a poisonous snake. Immediate application of lessons learned in jungle-survival training made possible his rapid recovery. At Trinidad's Edinburgh Field, where part of the ground party was customarily detailed to look out for snakes, two reptilian intruders were found one Tuesday morning. One was a coral snake, the other a fer-de-lance, neither anything to trifle with.

At one of ZP-41's bases, navy LTA was asked by navy HTA to help do something about a boa that had made its way up into the wheel well of one of the planes parked on the field. No amount of jabbing the uninvited visitor could make it leave or even move. The solution came not from the navy but from the natives who were looking on. They asked for some milk, put it in a bowl, and put the bowl under the airplane. A short while later Mr. Snake slithered his way down for the milk.

When yet another boa was discovered at Amapa, dispatched, and skinned, the detachment felt there should be some way of distinguishing it from the others. Taking their cue from the type-designation system in use by the Bureau of Aeronautics, they called it the XBC-1.

While this junglemania was going on, there was also a war in progress. Few, if any, U-boats remained in Brazilian coastal waters, but there were still "gray wolves" in the western part of the Caribbean. To counter them, ZP-23, hitherto at Hitchcock, Texas, was ordered to Vernam Field, Jamaica, in early 1944. Lieutenant Commander Cruse was detached from his duty in Trinidad to take com-

Amapa, Brazil and local workers. (U.S. Navy)

mand and take the squadron to its new operating area. He became commanding officer on 18 February 1944. On 8 March the first of ZP-23's airships landed at Vernam while the U.S. Army, Vernam being an army air base, looked on. The field was about thirty miles west of Kingston near the southern coast. The army helped the squadron get settled in, grading and building mooring circles and assisting in putting up masts. One was a telephone pole with a mooring cup on top.

The "new" ZP-23 had a detachment site at Barranquilla, Colombia. There were also sites at Mandinga, Panama, on the Caribbean side of the isthmus, and Chorrera on the Pacific side, about fifty and twenty miles, respectively, from the canal. Of all the advanced airship bases of World War II, Mandinga had to have been the worst. Amounting to little more than an airplane landing strip with a mast, it outjungled anything the squadrons in Brazil had to offer or put up with. One important difference, however, was that its snakes were bushmasters and pythons instead of boas. The heat, humidity, and isolation were enough to make one of the men of the detachment go berserk. He had to be subdued, straitjacketed, and evacuated. Another caught malaria and died.

Blimp operations began at Mandinga before they did at Chorrera. The airship that made the first flight between Vernam and Mandinga, an overwater distance of about 650 miles, had the squadron commander on board. The *K-60*, in its ferry flight from NAS Richmond to Vernam, had actually missed the island of Jamaica. So Cruse, taking no chances, accompanied the *K-60* from Vernam to Mandinga, partly to activate the detachment, partly to keep an eye on the navigation.

ZP-23 covered two sea frontiers. Vernam was in the Caribbean Sea Frontier, Mandinga and Chorrera in the Panama. Some of the escort missions flown out of Jamaica covered three hundred miles (six hours) to get to the rendezvous point. Saving enough fuel to get back meant that the ship could spend only three or four hours with the convoy. In the Panama area, ZP-23 chased practice torpedoes for American submarines when not flying antisubmarine missions.

ZP-23 could never claim direct contact with the enemy, but the Germans were not far away. On 11 July 1944 the *K-122* landed to pick up four out of fifteen survivors from a torpedoed tanker. While twelve miles offshore on a training flight, Lt.(jg) Willie J. Boehrs and crew sighted smoke and the light of a flare on the beach. Investigating, they found fifteen men, whose hand signals indicated that they had been torpedoed six days earlier and had come ashore there the night before. Boehrs looked the area over, decided he could safely land, and radioed the base his intent to do so. He picked a small clearing, two hundred yards long and fifty yards wide, that lay at right angles to the shore. Touching down, he disembarked his copilot, Ensign Lewis, to form a landing party of the survivors and to show them how to handle the lines on the next approach. On that second approach, two of the seamen were taken on board, those most in need of medical care. Boehrs then went around again, landed, and picked up two more. He took off, circled back, and landed once again to retrieve Lewis. The *K-122* then returned to base. Those survivors that it left behind, their whereabouts now known, awaited rescue by surface vessel. The four picked up by the *K-122* provided the first information available about the sinking of their ship.

Less than a week before, ZP-23 had found survivors of the *K-53*, which had flown into the sea the evening of 7 July.

The airships of a new squadron, ZP-24, would for a time fill the empty berths left behind by Blimp Squadron Twenty-Three when it departed Hitchcock, Texas, for Jamaica. ZP-24 was commissioned on 10 February 1944 and commanded by Lieutenant Commander Ayers, who had made the historic first rescue landing on the wheel the preceding year. Some weeks later, in June, ZP-24 would be transferred to NAS Weeksville so that ZP-14 could go overseas to Africa.

8. SEARCH AND RESCUE

NAVY AIRSHIPS WERE league-leaders in saving lives. They found survivors at sea, lowered provisions, summoned help, and stood by. They warned ships standing into danger and assisted those in distress. They helped plane crews who had ditched, even marking for a disabled Martin PBM flying boat a rock-clear area in which to make an emergency landing. They investigated so many plane wrecks that they took to marking them with paint so that they would not needlessly investigate them again.

Of the more than eighty search-and-rescue operations conducted by airships in 1944, two involved vessels with no one on board. The *K-46* sighted one, a small, hundred-foot, interisland banana boat, off Florida. Flying the U.S. flag upside down, it appeared undamaged, but it was empty. A half-mile away there drifted an empty lifeboat. A navy crash boat and a Coast Guard cutter, responding to the airship's call, confirmed that there was no sign of anyone and no ready explanation of why. The Coast Guard took the mystery craft in tow. In a similar case, an airship found a derelict with only a dog on board and no sign of a lifeboat anywhere. This latter proved to be the *Rubicon*, a vessel of about ninety tons that strong winds had swept, unoccupied, from her moorings in Havana Harbor.

Other lifesaving and lifeguarding incidents included locating and informing a merchant ship that one of its crew had been bitten by a dog found to be rabid, summoning a rescue boat to pick up teenagers whose sailboat had capsized, dropping medication for a seriously burned child, helping a destroyer out of Charleston rendezvous with a merchant vessel 120 miles away to take aboard a member of the Armed Guard who was ill with pneumonia, and notifying authorities of house and forest fires.

In early January 1944 the *K-36* and *K-98* of ZP-42 came upon four lifeboats and 107 men, survivors of two enemy blockade runners.

The *Rio Grande* had been trying to reach Germany from the Far East with rubber, ore, resins, and other strategic materials. The USS *Omaha* and *Jouett* had intercepted the blockade runner at 06°48'S, 025°36'W and sunk it with their gunfire on 4 January. A second runner, the *Burgenland*, was also sent to the bottom the next day at 07°29'S, 025°37'W. The German and Italian survivors had taken to the boats, but the American forces made no attempt to rescue the men because U-boats were thought to have been escorting the merchants.

With the action over, searching for the enemy lifeboats began. On the 7th and 8th surface vessels picked up two boats. Also on the 8th the *K-36* took off from Fernando de Noronha, ZP-42's "Rock

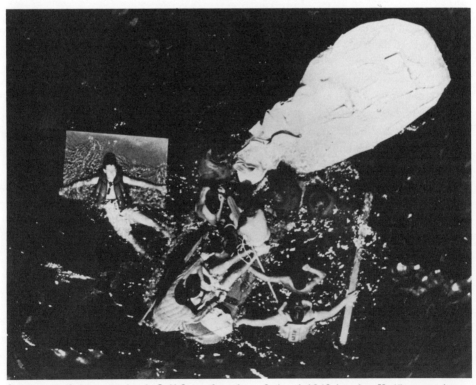

Survivors of the torpedoed *Gulf State*, found on 3 April 1943 by the *K-45*, struggle to inflate a life raft dropped by the airship. (U.S. Navy).

The *K-98* sights a boatload of twenty-six Germans and eight Italians, from a sunken blockade runner, off Brazil on 13 January 1944. (U.S. Navy Reproduced from Report on Airship Rescue Operations," Fleet Airships Atlantic)

Garden," and sighted a boat under sail. Then the *K-36* saw two more, eight and twelve miles away. The blimp advised its base of the find and was told to remain on station with the boats. The USS *Marblehead* was sent to the scene, homing on signals transmitted by the airship.

Meanwhile, the three boats, moving at different speeds, were separating. The *K-36*'s pilot, Lt. (jg) Cecil H. London, took his ship up to the lead boat and blinkered, "Halt Warten." The men in the boat responded by lowering their sail. London then approached the other two, signaling them by hand to rendezvous with the lead boat. Thus rounded up by the airship, the would-be blockade runners awaited rescue by the *Marblehead*, which asked the *K-36* to cover it while it picked the men up. There were seventy-three. When the airship landed at Maceio, it had been in the air for more than twenty-two hours.

The sixth and seventh lifeboats made it to land, coming ashore

117

at Fortaleza and south of Recife on the eleventh and thirteenth, respectively. It was on the thirteenth that the *K-98*, piloted by Ens. Eugene S. Pace, Jr., happened upon the eighth lifeboat. While covering convoy JT-19, the *K-98* sighted a boat under sail seven miles to the west, making about six knots. Pace advised the escort commander aboard the Brazilian minelayer *Comocim* and hovered above the boat until the thirty-four men aboard it were taken off.

The next day a merchant ship found the ninth and last of the boats, with fifty-two survivors. Over 250 enemy sailors had been rescued, airships accounting for 107 of them.

The story was not quite over, however. The enemy ships were gone, but not their cargoes. Bales of rubber dotted the sea. Two of ZP-42's ships were sent out to help local surface craft retrieve them.

On 11 February the *K-124* of ZP-51 scored a first for a K-ship. The squadron received a call asking for help finding an army launch, which was missing, unreported, and presumed in trouble.

The *K-124*, piloted by Ens. Sidney A. Verrier, was circling Trinidad's Edinburgh Field, preparing to land after being on patrol most of the day. At 1615 the airship was ordered to go look for the overdue launch. It found it at 1640. The boat, without engine power, was helpless and adrift in the Gulf of Paria, the wind and current taking it toward neutral Venezuela, where possible internment awaited the crew. Verrier throttled back. With a megaphone he called down to ask the half-dozen men on board what their situation was. They shouted back that they had no warm clothes, no food, and, worse yet, no life jackets. It was getting dark and the sea choppy. There being no surface craft within sight, Verrier decided to try towing them to safety.

No K-ship had ever towed an eight-ton launch before.

"We proceeded to rig our towing gear," Verrier later reported,

in the following manner: a rope bridle was rigged from the #2 frame of the car. By putting a serving six inches in length, four inches from the middle, we made an eye to which our tow line (drag rope and grapnel line) was bent. A piece of twenty-one thread approximately three feet in length was rove through both the shackle on the after outboard end of the car and the eye in the bridle so as to prevent the towline from damaging the rear doors of the car if and when the ship made a turn. A man was detailed to stand by to cut the tow line at once if it became necessary to drop the tow. Two marker buoys and a weight (a fruit can) were secured to the other end of the tow line. Rags were used on all places in the car where the rope came into contact to prevent chafing.

I put Ensign Hautman on the elevators with orders not to go below 150 feet at any time. Ensign Sweeney was on the rudder and Ensign Czarkowski stayed forward in order to coordinate the controls and relay my orders and directions. When all preparations had been made, we began our approach. When we were almost over the boat, we began to lower the line, but, because of the wind, they failed to get it. We went around again and this time lowered the line when we were a little forward of the launch. They secured the line to the king post that was forward in the boat. Besides securing it, they wound the line around the post two or three times. I was directing operations over the intercom system.

At 700 rpms we began to tow the boat steadily and gradually worked up to 950, at which time we were making twenty knots ground speed. We towed them for seven miles with ease. At that time the men in the boat attempted to lengthen the line by letting out the turns they had taken around the king post. They did this and the sudden snub that followed caused the line to part. We would have repaired and continued the operation but a surface craft had used the K-124 as a visible homing device and was now approaching. We decided to stand by and let it take the launch the rest of the way into port. At 1755, when the surface craft had the launch safely in tow, we departed.

All hands, especially the army, were delighted with this display of seamanship and airmanship. The incident was reenacted a couple of days later to photograph the towing technique that had been used. The versatility of naval airship crews and of the blimps they flew had been demonstrated once again. Commendations quickly followed. So did words of caution for other pilots who might try to do the same. For an airship to tow a surface craft could be a risky business. There was, of course, the obvious possibility that the strain could pull some of the structural members out of the car. There was also the chance that, when applying power to overcome the boat's inertia and get it moving, the blimp would be pulled downward and perhaps even into the water. The *K-124* was a late-model airship with rear-access double doors. The fact that the doorway faced directly aft, and not to the starboard side as on earlier models, had much to do with making the towing feasible.

119

The same day, 11 February, that ZP-51 came to the army's assistance in the Gulf of Paria, ZP-41 was doing the same for the army in the wilds of Brazil. Three B-25 Mitchell bombers were missing and believed down about sixty-five miles from Amapa. The *K-106* took off to look for them. It was carrying a pharmacist's mate, a rope ladder, machetes, axes, food, water, and small arms and ammunition, in addition to its usual flight personnel and gear. The jungle pickup of two Canadian fliers by ZP-41's airships only a week before had provided a lesson in how valuable this additional crew member and equipment could be.

The pilot, who was on the elevator wheel and wearing earphones while guarding the emergency frequency, suddenly heard, "Navy Blimp, Navy Blimp!" Those on the two downed planes—the third turned up safely elsewhere—had seen the *K-106*. The army pilots continued to call it, giving instructions about how to find them. Low cumulus overhung the area. Through a hole in the cloud cover, the men on the blimp could see flares and smoke. Ten minutes later the airship reached the spot to find that the two B-25s had belly-landed a hundred yards from each other. The voice on the radio advised that there were no injuries.

The *K-106* prepared to land. Boatswain John F. Desmond clambered down the rope ladder as the airship made a slow pass just a few feet above the ground. It was low enough for the propellers to strike and clip off some of the shrublike vegetation. Desmond dropped off, and the *K-106* revved its engines and began climbing. His job was to organize the ten survivors into a ground crew. Within fifteen minutes they had assembled with their belongings, had hacked down some of the taller bushes, and were awaiting the blimp's return. The ground was fortunately firm for the landing. The survivors' baggage was put on board. But under the tropical sun, the *K-106* began picking up superheat, so much so that the pilot had to break off the operation and take to the air.

His next try, according to ZP-41, was more successful:

A few minutes later a second landing was made. The Army men were lined up in V-formation. It was raining heavily but there was little wind and the airship remained relatively stable. The scene at this time was about as follows: In the background two downed bombers resting forlornly on their bellies. In the foreground a Navy blimp with its props turning over and occasionally hitting the bushes which came up as high as the bottom of the car at many points. On the airship's lines, a small group of rain-soaked men, happy over their impending delivery from near-disaster, and each now eagerly awaiting his turn to drop the line and make a dash around the props to the ladder at the door.

One by one, three of the Army men peeled off the lines and climbed on board. The operation was so well timed that, when the last man boarded, the blimp had enough way-on for control and yet not too much to prevent him from reaching the ladder. Two members of the airship's crew, in addition to Desmond, were left at the scene to compensate for those taken aboard.

While the *K-106* made for Amapa, the *K-114* arrived, landed, and picked up the remaining seven army fliers, at the same time depositing most of its own crew to join Desmond and the two other left-behinds. The *K-106* returned shortly afterward, finding its way back by the flares set off by Desmond. All loose and salvageable gear aboard the two airplanes had by this time been collected and was put into the car. Then the men on the ground climbed into the ship, Boatswain Desmond last. With everyone on, the blimp rolled through the bushes and took off. The next day the same airship returned to the crash site, this time to bring out machine guns and radio equipment from the planes.

All this took place, according to the squadron's report,

> in the heart of unbelievably dense jungle and thoroughly inaccessible. There are no rivers or trails in the vicinity and it is believed that, had it not been for the presence of the Navy blimps, the evacuation of the survivors could have been a matter of weeks, if possible at all. The Army survivors frankly stated that they felt they owed their lives to the blimp rescuers.

ZP-41's participants in this operation received Air Medals and commendations. Later on, ZP-41's airships revisited the area to deliver army personnel and supplies to attempt to salvage one of the airplanes.

Finding and extracting aviators from the jungle was big business to Blimp Squadron Forty-One. It flew hundreds of hours doing just that, being called upon whenever an airplane was missing in its operating vicinity. What airships offered, which no other aircraft at the time could, was the ability to search the jungle slowly, from a low altitude.

The Amapa-based *K-118* lands on the beach on 16 July 1944 to evacuate two army men stranded by the forced landing of their A-35. One makes his way toward the airship while two members of the blimp crew restrain it with the port short line and a third holds the car rail. (U.S. Navy. Reproduced from "Report on Airship Rescue Operations," Fleet Airships Atlantic)

Downed fliers would, of course, head for the nearest habitation they could find. For this reason, pilots searching for survivors paid a lot of attention to native villages, especially when their inhabitants waved to them. The trouble was that pilots were often unable to distinguish between when the natives were waving just to be friendly and when they were waving because they had something to tell.

Lt. (jg) Louis P. Reeder, formerly of ZP-15 and now with ZP-41, drew up a leaflet that was translated into Portuguese and was intended to be dropped on villages during searches for crash survivors. After explaining that an American airplane was down, it requested, "If anyone knows of, saw, or heard a crash, saw an American or knows of any such report, make the sign of a cross with wood, very large, and in a cleared space. If the airplane was not seen and no one knows of any report, make the letter 'A.'" Reeder selected this letter because it was easy to differentiate from a cross. Most of the locals could not read, but it was hoped that someone, a priest perhaps, would know how. Reeder's plan was soon put to the test when the *K-106* was checking on the reported sighting of a flare. When the pilot dropped the message to a village, the response on the ground was prompt and gratifying. After conversing animatedly between themselves, the natives began putting together an "A."

The lowering of a doctor to the seaplane tender USS *Lapwing* occurred when ZP-41 at São Luiz received a request on 21 August 1944 that penicillin and instructions for its use be air-dropped to the vessel for a man who had been running a temperature of 104 degrees for three days. Sulfa drugs had been given to him but had produced no improvement. Indeed, his condition appeared to be worsening. Acute appendicitis was suspected.

At 1005 the *K-88* took off with the squadron commander, Lt. Comdr. John J. McLendon, as pilot and Lt. Bryan St. J. Moynahan, Medical Corps, aboard. Moynahan wanted to go along so he could consult with the *Lapwing*'s pharmacist's mate about the patient's condition. Rendezvous was at 1140, and radio communication was established. The penicillin was lowered to the ship by a line. Talking with the pharmacist's mate, the doctor became convinced the seaman's condition was critical.

The *Lapwing* was a good seven or eight hours from port. Its captain, concerned that the ill man might not survive, asked if the doctor could come on board to treat him. Being lowered like the man on the flying trapeze was not exactly what Moynahan was used to. But he was a dedicated physician as well as a courageous one. He asked McLendon to put him on the ship. McLendon told him the risks. Moynahan persisted.

The crew put a parachute harness on the doctor, then secured it to the end of a 125-foot length of line they had cut from the drag rope. Then they put a life jacket over the harness. McLendon began his approach, keeping a steady altitude of one hundred feet. As the blimp crossed the ship's bow, the line, held by four men and with a turn taken around one of the structural elements of the car, was slowly let out. Moynahan was lowered away until he was only two feet above the water. At that point he let go and dropped in at a ground speed of about two knots. He went under and came up, inflating his life jacket as he surfaced. The *Lapwing* shot him a line, which he grabbed. The vessel, however, had difficulty maneuvering to pick him up. He was in the water for fifteen minutes before finally being hauled up on deck.

123

Moynahan found that the ill man did not have appendicitis. The doctor wanted to administer blood plasma, but there was none on the ship. He had, however, brought some from São Luiz, and it was still on the navigator's table in the *K-88*. He asked the airship to make a drop. The crew tied the plasma package to a line, lowered it away, and deposited it squarely on the tender. The plasma broke the fever, and the next morning the patient was much improved. For his actions, Dr. Moynahan received a commendation from Adm. Jonas H. Ingram, Commander Fourth Fleet.

Moynahan's demonstration of how a man could be lowered into the water on an improvised basis and without special equipment led inevitably to the question of what could be done on a prepared basis with special equipment. The result was the development of a rudimentary system whereby an individual, riding in a life ring with a canvas seat across it, could be lowered into the water or raised from it. This ring, a kind of aerial breeches buoy, had four supporting lines that converged into an eye. The line from the airship was connected to the eye.

Ring and man were let down or pulled up by a pulley arrangement—powered winches came later—in which detachable sandbags compensated for the weight of the load. Techniques were worked out to lower a life raft, provisions, and a rescue kit and to release them by a heavy sliding ring that dropped down the line and tripped the holding mechanism.

As the war neared its end, the navy's airships appeared increasingly likely to play a major air/sea-rescue role after hostilities ceased. The U.S. Coast Guard, in 1945, would send nine officers and thirty enlisted ratings to Lakehurst for flight training, anticipating that it would acquire some of the navy's K-ships after demobilization. It never did. The helicopter was coming of age. Its speed and maneuverability made it better suited for rescue missions. A good thing, the airship, gave way to a better.

9. THE AFRICA SQUADRON

⚓ IN FEBRUARY 1944 VPB-63, a squadron of PBY Catalina flying boats equipped with MAD was deployed to carry out magnetic barrier patrols across the Strait of Gibraltar. The vertical detection range of the equipment required that the "Madcats," as they were known, fly extremely low if they were to catch any U-boats attempting to enter the Mediterranean. This type of flying was demanding enough by day, especially fatiguing and dangerous by night.

Both Mills and Rosendahl believed that blimps should be used to relieve the PBYs by taking over their patrols during the hours of darkness. During one of his frequent visits to Washington, D.C., in the early spring of 1944, "Rosie" called on Comdr. George F. Watson of the Tenth Fleet.

The Tenth Fleet was a fleet without ships. It had been created in May 1943 to mastermind the defeat of Dönitz and his U-boats and win the Battle of the Atlantic. It had available to it information concerning enemy dispositions, capabilities, and intentions as gathered from the decryption of German naval communications, high-frequency direction finding on U-boat transmissions, ship and submarine plots, action reports, scientific and technical intelligence, and other sources. The Tenth Fleet oversaw the U.S. Navy's reponse to the U-boat "wolf packs" in midocean and the marauding of individual submarines in coastal waters. This fleet was a hush-hush operation. Not even its staff, located in the Navy Department in Washington, D.C., necessarily knew the sources of its information. The Tenth Fleet advised the Atlantic Fleet and the sea frontiers, sometimes informing, sometimes recommending, and sometimes directing. And when it directed, everyone jumped. The Tenth Fleet commander was no less than Admiral King.

On the staff of the Tenth Fleet in 1944, Commander Watson had previously served aboard the rigid airship *Los Angeles* and had established the first blimp squadron, ZP-32, on the West Coast on 31 January 1942.* By the late spring of 1943, Watson was ordered to temporary duty on the staff of Commander Fourth Fleet in Recife to select sites in Brazil for blimp bases and to negotiate the use of the Zeppelin hangar at Santa Cruz, southeast of Rio de Janeiro, with the Brazilian government.

Admiral Ingram gave Watson a Grumman JRF Goose to fly over the jungles, a Construction Corps officer from his staff, a Pan American Airways airport engineer on loan, a Brazilian navy legal officer, and Herbert Hoover, Jr., who was making a geological survey for the Brazilian government as part of a search for petroleum. Hoover proved invaluable in telling the team where water was to be found. In about six weeks sites had been selected between Amapa and Santa Cruz, and the use of the Zeppelin hangar had been agreed upon. The Fourth Fleet arranged for the construction work that followed.

While in Recife, Watson met two analysts from the Tenth Fleet who told him something about its nature, enough to convince him that he wanted to be part of it. Rosendahl was a Naval Academy classmate of Rear Adm. Francis S. "Frog" Low, the Tenth Fleet's chief of staff, and "Rosie" arranged for Watson to have an interview with Low, who took him on board and made him one of three in the Tenth Fleet's operations group.

When Rosendahl went to see Watson at Tenth Fleet headquarters, he told him he wanted an order to move blimps to Gibraltar released personally by King. "Frog" Low approved of the movement and wished Watson well. Approval was obtained from the French to base the airships at NAS Port Lyautey in French Morocco. There was concurrence, also, from the commander of U.S. naval forces in the area.

"I wrote the dispatch," Watson later recalled, "and a classmate, long-time Flag Secretary to King, made an end run that got me and my dispatch into Admiral King personally. King put his crooked 'K' on the message which allowed it to start with 'I direct . . .' This was the code that King himself had released it, words that made all concerned move fast."

126   * Airship operations along the Pacific Coast are described in appendix A.

Blimp Squadron Fourteen at Weeksville was selected to go to North Africa. Comdr. Emmett J. Sullivan was brought in from the West Coast to be the squadron commander. Enthusiastic, popular, and loaded with energy and ideas, "Sully" would quickly acquire the nickname of Captain Midnight, partly because of the secrecy surrounding his activities, partly because that was the name of the hero of a currently popular radio adventure series.

Overseas, ZP-14 would operate six airships. They would fly across the Atlantic in stages—NAS South Weymouth to NAS Argentia, Newfoundland; Argentia to Lagens in the Azores; the Azores to NAS Port Lyautey—and in pairs, starting with the *K-130* and *K-123*. Temporary stick or expeditionary masts, set in concrete and guy-wired for strength, would be available for them at Argentia and Lagens as they came through.

Eighty-four of ZP-14's personnel, twenty-two officers and sixty-two men, sailed from Norfolk, Virginia, on 17 May 1944 aboard the seaplane tender USS *Rehoboth*. Eleven days later they were followed by 174 more, 35 officers and 139 enlisted, who left New York on

The USS *Rehoboth* transported much of BlimpRon 14 to North Africa. (U.S. Navy)

the escort carrier USS *Mission Bay*. Aboard ship they helped stand communications and lookout watches and served galley duty.

At Terceira, the island of the Azores on which Lagens is located, a U.S. Army lighter off-loaded two masts and two hundred cylinders of helium for topping off the airships if they needed gas. Two officers, one of them an aerologist, and eight men went ashore to set things up and land the blimps when they arrived. Ten not being enough to make up a ground crew, use was made of the availability and willingness of a local construction battalion to help out.

From Lagens the *Rehoboth* went on to Casablanca, where it was joined a few days later by the *Mission Bay*. Squadron personnel and materiel were disembarked to begin the bumpy eighty-mile journey by truck to Craw Field, ZP-14's future operating site at NAS Port Lyautey.

After a flight of about sixteen hours, the *K-130* and *K-123* landed at Argentia on 29 May. The next morning they took off about 3,100 pounds "heavy," loaded to their maximum fuel capacity—1,180 gallons of gasoline and 36 gallons of oil—with a crew of nine.

The leg to Lagens took longer than twenty-one hours at an average airspeed of fifty-three knots, an average ground speed of fifty-eight knots, and a fuel consumption per airship of twenty-nine gallons per hour. Except for some rain and turbulence, the trip was uneventful.

There had been concern, however. The daily U-boat plot showed two of the enemy lined up right under the *K-130* and *K-123*'s projected track. Coincidence? Or were the Germans lying in wait? Stories that enemy radio broadcasts were reporting that the blimps were on their way heightened the concern.

Actually, there was no contact between the U-boats and the airships. The broadcasts were never confirmed. And Dönitz himself would later say that he had no advance knowledge that airships were making the crossing.

At Lagens, Sullivan boarded the *K-130* as pilot for the last leg. Lt. (jg) Homer B. Bly did the same for the other ship. Preceded by an army plane that flew ahead and reported the weather along the route, they arrived at Port Lyautey twenty hours later on 1 June at 1104 and 1123, with the *K-130* in the lead.

These were the first transatlantic flights by nonrigid airships. The distance in nautical miles from South Weymouth to Argentia was

The *K-130* lands at Port Lyautey, completing the first transatlantic flight by a nonrigid airship on 1 June 1944. (U.S. Navy)

782, from Argentia to the Azores 1,323, and from the Azores to Port Lyautey 1,040, making an overall total of 3,145 miles. Navigators for these flights were recent Naval Academy graduates because they were supposed to be expert at celestial navigation. They quickly found out, however, that the envelope overhead limited celestial shots to below thirty degrees. When they told Sullivan, his answer was, "They've got something new called Loran at MIT. Go there, check into it, and see if we can use it." So it was that Loran receivers were aboard ZP-14's airships when they flew the Atlantic.

The operations officer for the ferry movement was Lt. Comdr., perhaps by this time Comdr., Al Cope, formerly the commander of ZP-21 and now the chief staff officer to Commodore Mills. Cope was assisted by another of Mills's staff, Lt. John Dungan, a former enlisted aerographer's mate who, in 1944, was the aerology officer for Commander Fleet Airships, Atlantic. Dungan's role was crucial. The long midocean leg had to be flown with a tail wind. Dungan had to forecast it correctly, and he did.

129

The crew of the *K-130* immediately after the first landing at Port Lyautey. Standing (left to right) Ens. W. F. Gasner; Lt. (jg) E. J. Russell; Comdr. E. J. Sullivan; Lt. J. J. Barefoot; CBM L. Brodsky. Kneeling (left to right) ARM2/c H. E. Isreal, ARM1/c F. J. Platt, AMM1/c J. Grimaldi, AMM2/c W. Nicol. (U.S. Navy)

Philatelists would be disappointed to learn that, although the *K-123* carried letters, they bore no special cachet or cancellation marks. They were personal mail, collected at the last minute and put aboard for delivery to Port Lyautey.

Sullivan reported both airships ready to begin operational flying on 2 June, but assignment of the first mission was deferred to give time for local commands to be informed that airships were now on the scene. A certain amount of orientation about them was clearly called for. Few of the South African, French, British, and other Allied servicemen in the area had ever seen a blimp before. Some did not know what it was when they saw it.

Operations began with a one-airship mission the evening of 6 June, by coincidence D-Day. Two-ship operations at the Strait of Gibraltar began four days later. To relieve the PBYs at dusk, the airships took off at 1800, arriving at the patrol area a couple of hours later. They flew the barrier until dawn at a height of a hundred dred feet.

At that altitude, the slightest inattention on the part of the elevatorman could quickly put the airship into the drink. Flying in the
dark over water, he had few visual clues. To help him, the blimps
of ZP-14 carried radio altimeters that included a small display of
three lights, one green, one yellow, one red. The altimeter was set
for one hundred feet. At that height, the yellow light shone. Above
it, the green light came on. Below it, the red. Flying and watching
these lights was exhausting. Time on the elevators was broken up
by frequent reliefs.

The presence of two airships, blacked out under war conditions
and operating in the same patrol area, raised the possibility of collision, so they were permitted to fly the barrier with their running
lights on. The flights, from takeoff to landing, lasted about fifteen
hours.

On 15 June 1944 the *K-109* and *K-134* arrived, followed on 1
July by the *K-101* and *K-112*, all via the Argentia and Lagens route.
ZP-14 was now at full airship strength.

Six weeks after arriving in Africa, the *K-112* became the first U.S.
Navy airship to set down on the European continent since World
War I. The place was the Royal Air Force base at Gibraltar, where
a mast had been delivered and assembled. It was 18 July 1944.

The first airship patrol of the Strait of Gibraltar begins on 6 June 1944 with the *K-123*.
(U.S. Navy)

Landing at Gibraltar on 18 July 1944. (U.S. Navy)

Landing at Gibraltar was made difficult by the "spill" blowing over the Rock and by the proximity of the Spanish border. Through careful piloting, the *K-112* was able to keep clear of Spanish territory, set down on the wheel, and put its lines into the hands of fifty RAF men, none of whom had ever landed a blimp before. With the benefit of a blackboard lecture by one of ZP-14's officers who, with three of the squadron's enlisted men, was there to organize a ground crew, they proved themselves equal to the task. Two landings were made, the air vice marshal commanding the base taking a brief hop in between. After the second the ship was moored and refueled for its return flight to Port Lyautey. The test landing at Gibraltar was a success, but the subsequent nature of airship operations in the area never required another landing there.

Meanwhile, at Craw Field, everyone labored to make ZP-14's area suitable for flying, working, and living.

The assembly of the pyramid-shaped, red and white, mobile mooring masts was held up by damage suffered in transit by some of the structural members, by a lack of bolts and wrenches, and by the lack of identifying marks to be used in matching and piecing the parts together. As a consequence, operations were carried out from stick masts for longer than had been expected.

Maintenance shops were housed, to begin with, in tents. After about six weeks they were moved into Quonset huts, oblong, metal, shedlike structures with a cross section like a half-moon. Owing to malaria-carrying mosquitoes, most maintenance was done by day.

There were two helium-purification units, and these were put to work purging the *K-130*, removing air from its helium by passing the gas through charcoal. In twenty-four hours the ship's helium purity was raised from 93 percent to 95.5 percent.

Spare parts and supplies were stocked in a concrete warehouse just off the field. Items in short or nonexistent supply were borrowed from Construction Battalion Maintenance Unit 656, which turned out to be particularly accommodating in that regard.

Enlisted men lived five to a tent, all members of the same combat air crew. At first the junior officers lived in tents too, but later they moved into Quonsets holding eighteen to twenty each.

Mehdia Beach being not far away, officers rented a villa there as a place to sleep and rest after flying all night. Enlisted men, who had

To be an airship rigger, it helped to be an acrobat. AR1/c A. F. Trudeau checks the upper fin of the *K-130* (left) and replaces the tail wheel of the *K-101* (right). (U.S. Navy)

eight hours of liberty every third day, also visited the beach or spent their time in the city of Port Lyautey.

ZP-14, with six 250-foot-long airships to operate, quickly found its part of Craw Field too small and the flight approaches to it too cluttered with buildings and parked airplanes. In poor visibility the blimps had to thread their way through the congestion to a landing. So flight operations were relocated to another field, also small but free of obstacles. Then, in August, they were moved again to yet a third, one built just for LTA use. It was atop a small incline on the western side of the air station. Its oil-topped mat, 1,000 × 800 feet, had a short runwaylike extension at one end. Squadron offices and maintenance shops were located there. Because there was no blimp headquarters squadron at Port Lyautey, maintenance was performed by a unit of ZP-14 that called itself the aircraft service group.

Very early one morning, at about 0400 or 0500, Lt. Ben B. Levitt, ZP-14's duty officer, took a phone call. A voice said, "Admiral King

The operating mat specially constructed for LTA use at Port Lyautey. Squadron huts are clustered at its edge. At the lower right is "Helium Acres," the tent city housing ZP-14's enlisted personnel. (U.S. Navy)

is on base and on his way over to ZP-14." Levitt was tired, sleepy, disheveled, and in need of a shave, having been up all night, and he thought someone was pulling his leg. Admiral King? At that time of day? A few minutes later, a lone black sedan pulled up in front of the duty shack, and a tall, gaunt figure in blues got out. It was King! Except for the driver, he was by himself. He told Levitt he wanted to see Commander Sullivan.

"I'm sorry, Admiral, but he's not here. He's flying a mission."

"When will he be back?"

"In about three hours."

"I'll wait."

Whereupon King sat down, casting an appraising eye on Levitt and on everyone and everything in sight.

Levitt hurriedly sent a message to Sullivan: "ADMIRAL KING WAITING FOR YOU AT BASE X THIS IS NO JOKE."

He tried to find things to occupy King's time, offering him coffee and a tour through one of the airships on the field. King said he had already been in a K-ship. What promised to be a long three hours for Levitt were shortened considerably when the Admiral opened his briefcase and began going over paperwork.

When Sullivan returned, the nature of King's visit was clarified. He was not making a surprise inspection. He and Sullivan had apparently known each other for some time. He simply wanted to see "Sully" again and find out how things were going.

On 15 September two 3-pound rocks were sent hurtling into the envelope of the *K-101* as it sat moored on the field. A construction battalion blasting team, working five hundred feet away, had miscalculated. The accident took place at 1524. Fortunately, there were a lot of airshipmen around at the time to come to the rescue. All ballast was ordered taken off, the blower was started to keep up internal air pressure, the sleeve to resupply the bag with helium was rigged, and helium was added while the ship, losing gas and lift, was off-loaded. A ladder was put up against the side of the bag and another, a web ladder, draped over the top. Access to the top was from the masthead via a permanently rigged "man line" that ran from the bow to the tail. As the *K-101* struggled to survive, air was also blown into the helium chamber to keep the envelope from collapsing. The landing wheel was blocked so that the ship could not move, the car was propped up to relieve the bag of its weight, and the propellers were

135

Two rocks were blasted into the *K-101* on 15 September 1944. First aid, quickly rendered, saved the airship. (U.S. Navy)

taken off. Everything inside the car that could be removed was. The gas pressure dropped to one-quarter of an inch of water (one and a half inches was normal), The *K-101*, although badly wrinkled, pulled through, owing in no small part to the shirts stuffed into the holes to stop the leakage. By 1600 temporary patching had been completed. After an infusion of eighty thousand cubic feet of helium, the airship would return to service.

ZP-14's first serious flying accident occurred on 31 December 1944, seven months after the squadron's arrival in North Africa. It resulted in no injuries but considerable damage. While taking off, the *K-130* struck a dirt embankment at the edge of the field, bounced off it to a height of about forty feet, and continued on. The smell of gasoline quickly told its crew that the slip tanks under the floor had been damaged. So had the whole underside of the car. The wheel had been shoved up inside it. The radar hat was gone. The starboard propeller, having dug itself into the dirt, was bent. The skid along the bottom edge of the lower fin—skids replaced the everexpendable tail wheels at remote bases—was crushed. Some of the lower fin fabric was torn. The pilot ballasted the ship to land "light," there being no landing gear to take its weight. What he likely did not know was that he was carrying several hundred pounds of dirt that the blimp had scooped up from the embankment. The *K-130* got down on its third landing attempt damaging its washed-out underside a bit more and bending a blade of the other propeller. An emergency wheel, which ground crews kept handy, was attached so that the airship could be rolled up to the mast and moored. Some hours later strong gusts tore the emergency wheel away, and a dolly for wheeling about bombs was substituted for it. The aircraft service group repaired the damage.

The strategic picture in the Western Mediterranean had meanwhile changed enormously. Dönitz was no longer sending U-boats through the Strait of Gibraltar. An amphibious operation, Dragoon, had liberated the French ports of Toulon and Marseilles in August. With their capture had come a gigantic mine-cleanup job in their harbors. As a result of a conference between the Commander Eighth Fleet (Vice Adm. H. Kent Hewitt) and the Commander Fleet Air Wing Fifteen (Commo. G. T. Owen), under whom ZP-14 operated, it was decided to send an airship to Toulon to try it out for minesweeping work. The *K-112* was selected.

On 13 September an R5D transport plane was made available to take eight blimpron officers, fourteen enlisted men, a stick mast, and some ancillary gear to the former French naval airship station at Cuers, eleven miles northeast of Toulon. Given twelve-hours notice, they were on their way.

In the 1920s Cuers had been to the French navy what Lakehurst had been to the American: the center of its rigid airship activity. The spoils that France acquired from Germany after World War I included four Zeppelin hangars that had been dismantled, brought to Cuers, and re-erected as two. Each of the two was 770 × 150 × 197 feet. They had housed France's *Mediterranée* and *Dixmude*, Zeppelins seized from the former enemy.

With Sullivan as pilot, the *K-112* arrived at the French base on 17 September after having landed to a hurriedly erected stick mast at Oran, Algeria, remaining there overnight, and starting out again before dawn under instrument conditions. At Cuers members of an Australian Spitfire squadron landed the airship.

Operations at Cuers began on 21 September with the spotting and plotting, not the sweeping, of moored mines. Using visual bearings and radar bearings and distances, it was found that the mines

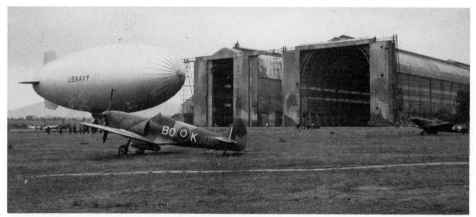

The *K-112* on the field at Cuers-Pierrefeu. The Spitfires shown were flying strafing missions against the Germans at that time of the war. (U.S. Navy)

could be seen and their positions accurately plotted. Seven of the silent menaces were detected the following day in the inner harbor of La Ciotat Bay. Near St. Mandrier Point, twenty-one more were seen and mapped.

On the 24th mine-spotting operations were suspended so that the *K-112* could fly an MAD patrol across the entrance of Toulon's habor. Warnings had been received of imminent attacks on shipping there by enemy torpedo boats and midget submarines. The *K-112* flew an MAD "fence" from 1900 to 0900 that night and the night following. The attacks never materialized.

The airship photographed Toulon harbor on the 29th to help authorities assess the extent of damage to its installations. That same day it plotted a field of 120 mines.

Two days later the *K-112*, in company with three minesweepers, investigated an area in which there were believed to be undiscovered mines. It sighted two, marked them with smoke floats, and, using a loudspeaker, directed the surface vessels to them. This was the beginning of active airship cooperation with surface minesweeping craft. The blimp communicated with the ships by loud hailer or radio, carrying a French officer on board to handle linguistics.

Returning to La Ciotat Bay and operating there from 13 to 15 October, the *K-112* spotted more than a dozen moored contact mines for surface craft to cut loose and destroy by gunfire. The Commander Escort Sweeper Group found the blimp to be of great assistance, pointing out that it had warned one of the sweeps, which was unsuspectedly bearing down on a mine, to change course. The airship did not attempt to sink any mines itself with its machine gun, leaving that to the surface units.

There was a squadron change-of-command ceremony on 19 October. Commander Sullivan was detached to become Air Group Commander (LTA) on the staff of Commander Fleet Air Wing Fifteen. His relief was Lt. Comdr. Franklin S. "Ibby" Rixey, who came from Lakehurst, where he had commanded ZP-12. The Germans, apparently miffed because they had not been invited to the ceremony, overflew Cuers the next night and dropped flares around the *K-112* as it lay moored out on the field.

What was it like at Cuers where until recently German dive-bomber units had been based? Lt. (jg) Richard C. Kline was there and wrote this description in his picture-and-text official history *ZP-14 Overseas*:

> French and British units at Cuers cooperated wholeheartedly in the establishment of blimp facilities on the field. Australian "fitters" (mechanics) provided fueling facilities until their squadrons departed.
>
> Twenty-two hundred land mines were reportedly removed from the field and vicinity before it became operational for Allied aircraft 29 August. As late as the middle of October, German prisoners were still de-mining vineyards surrounding the aerodrome. Three Spitfire squadrons were flying strafing missions from the field when the K-112 arrived. A French squadron of Walruses occupied one of the two hangars. Blimpron storerooms were located in it.
>
> German soldiers who had been captured near Cuers a few weeks before aided flight crews in ground handling operations. These prisoners were used only for handling and docking. Flight crews ground handled the ship on takeoffs. Occasionally a single cigarette was given to each German and French guard after completion of a landing. On moonless nights, flashes believed to be from artillery on the Italian front could be seen by pressure watch standers.
>
> Selection of one of the docks for use automatically resulted in naming it Dock #1, the doors of which were put into operation 18 September for the first time in years. Before the hangar was prepared for use, a mine disposal officer inspected it thoroughly for booby traps. Nothing was found. French civilians aided in clearing

years of accumulation of debris. Machinery designed to operate the doors was inoperative. An American tank had lobbed some shells which put holes in the doors but these did not interfere with the opening operation or do any damage inside. Opening and closing the doors became a five-minute operation using a cable and block rigged to a tractor.

Lack of a mobile mast made docking operations risky. A mobile mast did not arrive until the last week in October. When it was time for its 120-hour check, the K-112 was docked for the first time, 3 October, in practically calm wind conditions. The hangars have doors on the east end only. For daily operations, the ship was kept on the mast except when Mistral winds of gale force were predicted. Because of the lack of aerology units close by during the first weeks' operations, the K-112 rode out three such storms.

Ring bolts along the sides and in the deck of the hangar were adapted easily to the mooring lines of the K-112. A twenty-five-foot rigid airship work platform was in good condition and used for inspection of nose and tail assemblies. Trim of the ship was altered to bring the bow or stern down within reach of the platform. A trough along the centerline of the hangar deck simplified the problem of keeping the airship's wheel centered. Water was piped into the hangar but there were no electrical connections.

Communications with other commands were carried out first by courier or directly from the airship while it was on the mast. This latter method proved impractical during high winds or when the ship was in the hangar. Late in October, equipment was set up in a radio shack built by crew radiomen to operate on the frequencies used during flight. A VHF set from a Spitfire was installed in the K-112 during the period that British aircraft operated from Cuers; this was to make possible communication with the tower on the field. A Navy aerology unit was established in that tower during the second week in October.

Living at Cuers during the first weeks was under field conditions. For a few days, food consisted of Army "C" and "K" rations. All gear was transported from Port Lyautey by plane. Lavatory facilities consisted of outside artesian wells. Commander Sullivan, as did all hands, washed his own clothes. During spare moments, [land] mine-wary crews went souvenir hunting. Fireplace wood was obtained from German foxholes.

Officers lived in a villa formerly occupied by German officers. A French farm family occupied part of it. There was electricity but no other modern conveniences. When the *K-109* arrived 24 October, an-

At left, one of the two villas occupied by ZP-14's officers at Cuers. At right, housing shared by its enlisted men with those of the French navy. (U.S. Navy)

other villa was obtained. Enlisted men lived in one section of the French enlisted men's barracks and ate there. Officers, who were helped by two French domestics, cooked their own meals. Later the first villa became Senior Officers Quarters; all meals for officers were prepared and served in it. Located a half-mile away, the second villa, the one for junior officers, was more modern, with running water, inside toilet, and galvanized metal bath tub. Both villas were heated by fireplace. Each officer took turns at holding 0630 reveille and going to collect the German prisoner and French help who did the housework.

The Ship's Service consisted of a single locker from which rations were issued weekly. One can of beer daily, five packages of cigarettes weekly, a couple of packages of gum, and candy made up the usual ration.

Shortly after it reported to Cuers for duty, the *K-109* was sent to Bizerte, Tunisia, to fly mine-spotting missions out of Sidi Ahmed Field. A stick mast was brought in by PBY and R5D aircraft, and the airship itself arrived on 3 November. It stayed for a little over two weeks, then moved on to Cagliari, Sardinia, for more of the same. It left to the surface sweepers and "sink boats" the job of destroying the 268 mines it sighted during its first three flights over the harbor. It did use its .50-caliber machine gun to sink net buoys, however. ZP-14's Cagliari detachment would stay on until spring despite the steady diet of Sardinian cauliflower to which it was treated in the British mess that it shared. Its four flight crews were

141

At Cuers the men prepared to receive the enemy at the time of the attempted German breakthrough in December 1944. (U.S. Navy)

Emmett J. Sullivan receives the Legion of Merit from Commander Fleet Airships, Atlantic for deploying Blimp Squadron Fourteen overseas. (U.S. Navy)

also dependent upon British communications and aerological support.

Late December brought the final, all-out German land offensive of the war. Although centered in the Ardennes in Belgium, it had an impact that extended to southern France. When German parachutists, speaking English and wearing American army uniforms, were captured near Toulon, Cuers went on full alert. Squadron officers wore sidearms. The machine guns of the *K-112* and *K-134*—the latter arrived during the first week in December to relieve the former, which was due for an engine change—were set up inside the hangar. Everyone practiced his marksmanship. The French Resistance stopped and detained a squadron officer who found himself outside the base after dark.

After the offensive failed, Cuers resumed operating as before. From the home base, eight hundred miles away, ZP-14's airships continued their magnetic patrols of the Strait of Gibraltar.

10. SERVICES RENDERED

⟁⟁⟁ ATLANTIC FLEET AIRSHIPS performed many types of utility services. These missions included searching for sunken vessels; clearing shipping from danger areas; looking for barges parted from their tows; checking aids to navigation; surveying the coastal blackout; mapping government property; picking up and delivering mail, equipment, and personnel in isolated areas; and looking for smuggler hideouts overseas. Especially important, the airships took pictures.

Blimps were, and still are, tremendous camera platforms. Airship squadrons were proud of their photography and vied with one another to have the best photo department. Had there been a formal competition, the winner would almost certainly have been Weeksville's ZP-14 and its photographic officer, Lt. (jg) Richard C. Kline. A former newspaperman, he infected his squadron with such enthusiasm for photography and for the K-20 aerial camera (no relation to the airship *K-20*) that by early 1944 ZP-14's crews had taken 4,500 pictures of more than 800 different types of vessels. These shots were much in demand for briefing purposes by Eastern Sea Frontier headquarters and by the editors of the training publications that dealt with ship recognition.

The first realization that airships could be useful for taking motion as well as still pictures seems to have come from a Bureau of Aeronautics project to make a training film in the Straits of Florida. The film was intended to show how a flier should inflate and use his life raft after a ditching. Attempts to shoot the film from an airplane did not work out because its wing tips kept intruding into the camera's field of view. The straits being an airship operating area, the bureau requested camera help from ZP-21 at Richmond. The filmmakers were evidently pleased with the results because other requests quickly followed. The squadron complied as best it could,

144

learning after some trial and error that one of the best places to put the camera was in the machine-gun turret.

In one scenario, the aerial maneuvering of a late-model fighter was to be filmed. ZP-21 gave the assignment to its *M-3*, which dutifully carried it off not far from the eastern coast of Florida. The plane zoomed, buzzed, and barrel-rolled around the blimp, looking for all the world like it was attacking it. People on the beaches, who were not accustomed to seeing an M-ship, which was half again larger and looked very different from a "K," took it for a German Zeppelin. Thus originated the story that a navy plane had attacked a Zeppelin near Miami.

So frequent and numerous were the requests for blimp photographic or other services that on 10 February 1944 Commander Fleet Airships, Atlantic established Airship Utility Squadron One, also known as AirUtRon One or ZJ-1. Lt. Comdr. Marion H. Eppes, thin, sandy-haired, and personable, was its commanding officer. Eppes had qualified as a naval aviator (airship) before the war, completed a tour of sea duty in the Pacific, and commanded ZP-23 at Hitchcock, Texas.

An M-ship in flight. (U.S. Navy)

145

ZJ-1 was headquartered at Meacham Field, Key West, Florida, later to become that city's international airport. It had a detachment at NAS South Weymouth and subdetachments at Elizabeth Field on Fisher's Island, New York; the Naval Proving Ground, Dahlgren, Virginia; and the Naval Mine Warfare Test Station, Solomons, Maryland.

Elizabeth Field was perhaps the most unusually named naval Facility of World War II. The officer-in-charge, curious about the name, decided to investigate who Elizabeth was. It turned out that Elizabeth had been a mule! For years the field had been her pasture. After she died, it had continued to be known as her field. To the credit of the navy, it accepted that fact and never tried to deprive Elizabeth of her legacy. Elizabeth Field it was and Elizabeth Field it remained as long as the blimps were there.

The creation of the utility squadron coincided roughly with the phasing out of wartime LTA flight training. The number of pilots available was now adequate for the airships on hand. L-ships and

G-type airships were converted from training to utility work. (U.S. Navy)

G-ships, heretofore used for training, became available for reassignment. ZJ-1 opted for the "Gs." Pilots accustomed to the "Ks" had to get used to these smaller (196 thousand cubic feet) and slower (forty knots cruising) ships, which while not as sturdy had a tighter turning circle and better maneuverability for utility work.

At least two L-ships were sent to operational squadrons for general use, one to ZP-11 at South Weymouth and one to ZP-14 at Weeksville.

The utility squadron's Detachment #1 at South Weymouth serviced the Gould Island Range of the Naval Torpedo Station at Newport, Rhode Island. Torpedoes, 80 to 120 per day, were fired from a pier down a 10,000-yard range into Narragansett Bay. The airship, in voice radio contact with the pier, reported the track and location of each torpedo as it surfaced at the end of its run. Retriever boats, acting on this information, recovered the expended "fish." If a torpedo sank, the blimp marked the location of the air bubbles with a smoke float. Divers later went down for it.

These torpedo-tracking operations were difficult to carry out because pilots had to keep one eye on the shots and the other on the air traffic. The range was at the eastern edge of the traffic pattern of NAS Quonset Point. G-ship pilots, much to their consternation, could find as many as twenty or thirty aircraft flying within a half-mile of them. The pilots personally handled communications at the range, and one of the ship's two receivers was tuned to the range frequency, the other to the Quonset tower. The South Weymouth frequency was left unguarded, communications to and from the home base being relayed through Quonset Point.

Chasing torpedoes fired by submarines in the Block Island Sound area was handled differently and was the job of the subdetachment at Fisher's Island. There was no range as such. Submarines launched torpedoes from periscope depth at moving targets. Instead of using radio to communicate the blimps and submarines used blinker light and a system of prearranged signals meaning "firing completed," "return to base," and the like. Airship crews had to be alert to recognize launch bubbles, wakes, and periscope feathers because they marked the firing point. There would be seven or eight torpedo launchings a day, sometimes hours apart. When there were long delays, the G-ship proceeded to Fisher's Island, normally about fifteen miles away, landed, waited them out, and then returned. About five hundred yards from the target ship and below five hundred feet in altitude, it would track the shot, marking the end of its run with flares for the retrieval boat. Torpedoes were launched with the submarine submerged by day and on the surface at night. For nighttime tracking and recovery, a flare was carried in the torpedo's nose.

Joint operations led to a certain amount of camaraderie between the airshipmen and the submariners. And with camaraderie came horseplay. Airshipmen liked to scare the wits out of unsuspecting passengers making orientation flights by suddenly cutting back the engines during a climb. In an airplane this meant "curtains," but in an LTA craft it meant only that the airship would settle into a floating mode, sinking or rising slowly depending on whether it was "heavy" or "light." Some submariners, given this treatment, vowed to exact a fit form of retribution.

The time and opportunity came when it was the airshipmen's turn to make an orientation dive in a submarine. The submariners were eager and ready to return all favors. They staged a casualty and abandon-ship drill without telling their poopy-bag guests that it was all make-believe. Then they informed the airmen that they would have to don escape lungs and ascend to the surface through a hatch. As the color drained from the LTA personnel's faces, the submarine boys took pity, opened up the hatches, and let the sunlight stream in. According to one version of this oft-told tale, the blimp men, when they went out on deck, found that the submarine was tied to the dock and had been so all along.

The subdetachment at Dahlgren worked the range at Piney Point, Virginia, where the Potomac River enters the Chesapeake Bay, for the Naval Torpedo Station, Alexandria, Virginia. Nothing very noteworthy marked these operations, which were carried out by G-ships and their usual crew of two pilots, a radioman, and a mechanic. There could be some interesting moments, however, arising from the gunfire at Dahlgren, which could make the blimp shake at its moorings and the stick mast vibrate. One day a particularly sharp report cracked the glass of the clock on the pilot's instrument panel.

Missions flown at the Mine Warfare Test Station, Solomons, Maryland, and for the Underwater Explosion Research Laboratory of the Woods Hole (Massachusetts) Oceanographic Institute were mostly photographic. A camera mount, developed at South Weymouth, enabled pictures to be shot from the side of the car rather than only from its forward end. This mount made it possible for the blimp to take pictures while circling and eliminated the need to keep the airship constantly pointed at the subject. On these flights an F-56 camera, with a seven-and-a-quarter–inch lens, was used. A hand-held motion-picture camera, with a four-inch lens, was also employed. Because both the still-and motion-picture photographers took their shots while their feet were dangling outboard, a safety harness had to be devised for them.

When the daily photographic missions for Woods Hole ended in the summer of 1944, they were replaced by missions flown for scientists of the Massachusetts Institute of Technology. All that the "brains" from MIT ever said about their work was that they were examining the effects of weather on electronic-wave propagation. They would arrive when they considered the weather "right," board the airship with about two hundred pounds of gear, and then depart in silence and secrecy after the flight was completed.

For a while a G-ship flew daily from South Weymouth to Brenton Reef in Block Island Sound to photograph torpedoes launched at target vessels by units of the Motor Torpedo Boat Training Center, Melville, Rhode Island. Often the blimp carried officers from the training center to oversee the operation. The launching boat would call the blimp to ask how the shot went, the airship replying while it raced after the dummy weapon to mark it for retrieval.

A mission that increased in importance and frequency was the calibration of shipboard and shore-based radio direction finders and radars. Utility airships literally flew in circles while ships and stations kept the blimp visually in sight and compared the visual bearing to it with the radio or radar bearing and, in the case of the latter, with the distance as well.

To provide realistic experience and advanced training in the latest antisubmarine techniques, Fleet Airships, Atlantic maintained an Airship Antisubmarine Training Detachment, Atlantic Fleet at Meacham Field. Utility Squadron One operated this Key West training activity and the two K-ships assigned there for the purpose. The activity was housed in East Martello Towers, a five-sided U.S. Army fort built a century earlier.

149

"Meacham Tech" offered a three-week cram course in airship antisubmarine fundamentals: one week of classroom work inside the casemates of the fort; one week of flying aboard the K-ships for instructional purposes; and one week of going to sea aboard the escorts and submarines with which students had been exercising in Key West waters. Later the course would be expanded to send combat aircrew commanders to the local Fleet Sound School to learn more about sonar and to practice tactics on the "attack teacher."

The LTA facility at Meacham was known for its good flying weather, its proximity to cooperating ships and submarines, and its thriving canine population. Most airship units had a collection of mutts to whom all sorts of phenomenal feats were attributed—like helping pull on the handling lines and biting only officers, never enlisted men. Normally, Meacham's collection of strays got along well together, but the day Commodore Mills came to visit, he was treated to the greatest canine free-for-all ever.

Airship Antisubmarine Training Detachment, Atlantic Fleet would be disestablished on 27 May 1945, Airship Utility Squadron One about two weeks later on 9 June. During 1944 and until 15 May 1945 ZJ-1 made 814 torpedo-recovery, 171 photographic, and 44 radio-or radar-calibration flights.

11. LIVES LOST

~~~~ THE FIRST ATLANTIC FLEET airship flight fatality took place on 18 July 1943 when the *K-74* was shot down and one of its crew died in the water.

The next death occurred on 16 October 1943 when, in fog along the New Jersey shore, the *K-64* collided with the lower stabilizer of the *K-7* a half-mile north of Barnegat Inlet. The accident took place at 0950 as the *K-64* of Squadron Twelve moved south down the beach before heading seaward to its patrol area. The *K-7* belonged to the Airship Training Squadron at Lakehurst, the activity that provided advanced training on K-ships for the Naval Airship Training and Experimental Command. As the *K-64* came down the coast, the *K-7* was circling Barnegat Lighthouse. The ceiling was zero, and visibility was zero to two hundred feet.

The pilot of the *K-7* was aft in the car when the two airships came together:

> A severe shock shook the ship and at the same time our tail dropped suddenly. At the instant of the shock, I looked up and saw the bow of a K-ship in contact with our tail. As I looked, this ship's bow dropped and seemed to pull our tail with her. I flung open the rear door, turned forward to the crew, and gave the command to prepare to abandon ship. There was a second and less severe shock at this time. I turned to see the other ship fall free of us. We were at 250 feet. The other ship dropped as a dead weight. Its bag was in ribbons.

Aviation Machinist's Mate 2nd Class H. C. Hunter was the sole survivor of the nine men aboard the *K-64*:

> All at once we felt a little jerk and the whole ship shuddered. Everybody sat up on their seats. I was sitting on the starboard side

just forward of the door, and when I sat up I was looking straight forward and saw the pilot giving down elevator. Then there was a big crash and a rip and I could see the edge of the bag going by the window. Just momentarily we paused, I jumped out of my seat, and then the car tipped aft. I started toward the door. I tried to get the safety bar up and by that time we were in the water. When we hit, I was knocked down, as was everybody else. I remember struggling up and I had a hold on the safety bar. By this time I could see bright orange in the car and it was burning. I grabbed Giordano. He was wedged in against the seat. He wasn't moving. I tried to inflate his life jacket. I tried to move him. Then I had to get out.

The door was forced open by the water and I pulled myself out and inflated my jacket. When I hit the surface, there was a little fire. I looked up and the bag was lying right over me, so I ducked under and swam out. There was a little ring of fire and I was in it. I got a breath of air and then I ducked under and swam out of this ring of fire and came up just on the edge of it. I swam about thirty feet. I heard a dull rumble. Some gas must have exploded. There was a big sheet of fire behind me about fifteen feet high starting to spread out and it was nip and tuck whether I was going to get away. Finally I got about sixty feet away from it and stopped to rest. I looked back but couldn't see anybody. Just a bag in flame and smoke. So I headed toward the beach and finally made it.

Hunter had first degree burns on his hands and feet and a sprained left knee. He was helped ashore by people on the beach who had heard the collision and saw the fire and wreckage. Two went to the Forked River Coast Guard station for help. A Coast Guard picket boat began a search for survivors, and Coast Guardsmen patrolled the beach off which the *K-64* lay. The surf washed most of it ashore.

In the poor visibility, the *K-64* had struck the static discharge rod at the base of the *K-7*'s lower fin. This aluminum rod, about six inches long, had cut into the *K-64*'s bag and sliced it open, bringing it down into the Atlantic two hundred yards from shore. The *K-7* returned safely to base. The accident's cause: the failure of the controllers at Lakehurst to advise the pilots that they were on collision courses.*

* In addition to the casualties suffered by airships of the Atlantic Fleet, three major accidents took place to LTA craft operated by NAS Lakehurst. The *G-1* and *L-2* collided on 8 June 1942 with a loss of twelve (see chapter 2). A hydrogen-inflated free balloon was ignited by static electricity when its rip cord

Also in October 1943 the *K-94*, an airship from ZP-51 on a ferry flight from Guantanamo Bay, Cuba, to San Juan, Puerto Rico, burned in midair the night of the thirtieth. The blimp was totally consumed. Its pilot was Lt. (jg) Wallace A. Wydeen, who was introduced to the reader via the *K-68* in chapter 6. It was 2230. Visibility was good. The *K-94* was being tracked by army radar at San Juan. Its blinking navigation lights were seen by a cable ship, the *Eduoard Jeremac*, and by the subchaser *SC-1304*. Three officers and five enlisted men were aboard the airship.

Suddenly, a small flaming object was seen to drop from the *K-94*. Then the blimp became illuminated in a bright glow, yellowish-orange or red. The airship fell toward the water, a large burst of flame enshrouding it as it neared or struck the surface. The flames died out, and black smoke followed.

From eight miles away the *SC-1304* and *Eduoard Jeremac* made for the scene. They found only a radar spare-parts box burning in the water, some packing material, and a fragment of an instruction sheet that may have come from the box.

Nothing else . . . no airship wreckage . . . no survivors or bodies. There was a strong smell of gasoline in the air.

To compound the tragedy, an army B-25 sent out from Borinquen, Puerto Rico, to assist crashed within sight of the subchaser.

There had been no enemy action. No gunfire had been heard, and there had been no explosion. Somehow the *K-94* had self-destructed. In the absence of survivors or meaningful wreckage, it was impossible to determine how. Its radio operator, unable to reach NAS San Juan by voice, had been sending in Morse with a hand key. Sparks from the contact points of the key could have ignited gasoline fumes if there were any in the car. And if Wydeen had been transferring fuel at the time, there would have been some. But Wydeen was experienced and competent and knew that electrical gear was to be secured when shifting fuel. What was the flaming object seen to drop from the car? It could have been a full slip tank with a small flame burning at its opening. No one would ever know.

---

was pulled during a landing. That fire killed three in 1943. A training airship, the *K-5*, failed to clear the door of Hangar #1 while practicing takeoffs and landings on 16 May 1944. The ten dead included the author's close friend, Lt. McCain Smith, whose widow, Helen, would later become press secretary to First Lady Mrs. Richard Nixon.

The fire that destroyed the *K-94* in midair was never explained. The investigation centered about the possible ignition of gasoline, which was carried in overhead tanks inside the car (left). Fuel was transferred between tanks in flight (right). (U.S. Navy)

On 19 April 1944 the *K-133* of ZP-22 was forced down in the Gulf of Mexico in an accident many had feared would someday come. It was destroyed by a thunderstorm. There had been a number of close calls as K-ships had been carried violently up and down in the vertical currents of these disturbances. No squadron's airship, however, had thus far been destroyed by one. Indeed, until the destruction of the *K-133*, no Atlantic Fleet airship had ever been lost in flight because of the weather.

The *K-133* unknowingly entered a thunderstorm while flying at 550 feet in visibility that was nil. For forty-five minutes it was carried up and down—at one point to eleven thousand feet—before crashing into the gulf at 1035.

Eight of the ten crew members got out of the car safely. In the strong winds and rough water, the airship's life raft parted its line and drifted out of reach. The eight stayed together but, although wearing life jackets, died one by one in the rough water. Only Ens. William Thewes was alive when rescue came.

According to Thewes,

> We had a blur about ten miles around on the radar scope. We went up to 7,000 feet and the pressure rose to four inches and went down to 4/10 of an inch. We came down to 5,000 feet and the pressure dropped to zero. We never did get it up after that. Ballonets held pressure but they were the only thing. We had the mixture running at full rich. Then we bounced around between 5,000 and 8,000 feet. Once we were at 10,000 feet and there was snow there. During that time, we dropped our bombs and slip tanks and all but 370 gallons of fuel. Told to get the confidential gear ready to throw out, I went at the MAD first while the rest of the men were ripping up the aft section of the car. When we got all the boxes loose, we sent them aft so they could be handled quickly. Sometime during this period, the oil pressure dropped and information was radioed in with our position.
>
> We hit as high as 11,000 feet. We started to rip up the radar. We began to go down. At about 7,000 feet, we got the order to throw everything out. At 1,500 feet, the order was given to break out the liferaft. By now everything had been thrown overboard except the radar box and we decided to jettison it out the door behind the rudderman. Due to the angle of the car, we slid backwards and stopped at the Lawrance Power Unit. The order was then given to stand by to hit the water so we braced the radar box in front of the Lawrance as we hit. The engines, when they stopped at 7,000 feet, were re-started; when they stopped again at 700, they were not.
>
> The tail fin hit first. We were going backwards very fast. The rear doors were open and the water rushed in.

ZP-11's *K-14* flew itself into the water on 2 July 1944 while conducting an MAD search near Bar Harbor, Maine. Altitude was between 200 and 250 feet when the copilot, having just relieved the man on the elevators, diverted his attention from the altitude and began to adjust the intensity of the ultraviolet light illuminating the instruments. There was no forward lookout in the bombardier's position. Without anyone noticing it, the *K-14* was nosing down and losing altitude. When, at last, someone saw how close the water was and called out, it was too late. Into the sea went the airship.

There was the wrenching sound of metal being bent and broken. Then the gurgling of seawater as it entered the car. Five men man-

155

aged to get out, the fifth becoming separated from the others and disappearing. When the car was recovered, it was found that its outboard bombs were missing and that the arming wires were in place, meaning that they had been armed when they left the ship. The envelope, when salvaged, was torn aft and had its stern ripped away. Investigators concluded that the bombs had gone off after impact upon sinking to their fifty-foot settings. An Army boat picked up the four survivors. The bodies of the remaining six were recovered.

The *K-53* (of ZP-23 out of Vernam Field, Jamaica) flew into the Caribbean the evening of 7 July 1944. Nine of its crew of ten were rescued after two days adrift on two life rafts. The tenth man vanished at the time of the crash and was never found. In fact, the survivors came close to not being found. An Army B-25 spotted their rafts the afternoon of 8 July, making three passes over them and then

The *K-53* after crashing into the Caribbean. One crew member was lost. (U.S. Navy)

losing them. Not until the afternoon of the ninth, despite an intensive search, would they be sighted again by another of ZP-23's airships, the *K-60*, piloted by Lt. (jg) Gordon E. Burke.

Burke counted the nine survivors in the rafts—they were in generally good condition except for severe sunburn—and radioed that information plus their position to base. Then he descended to about fifty feet to drop water, rations, and cigarettes. He also lowered flares for them to use in case they were not picked up by nightfall. But the flares were not needed. Less than four hours later the USS *Unimak*, which had been searching the area, arrived on the scene.

The only other Atlantic Fleet airship of the war to crash in flight with fatalities was the *K-34*, another of ZP-11's ships that flew into the sea. Human error was the officially assigned cause but, according to the pilot, icing that obscured visibility had been a contributing factor. The accident took place on 10 November 1944. Two lives were lost. The opinion of the *K-34*'s pilot notwithstanding, it appears that no airship was lost in the Atlantic during the war as a direct result of icing.

Seven airships lost with a total of thirty-five fatalities—and five of the ships lost ended in "4" (the *K-14, K-34, K-64, K-74,* and *K-94*).

Considering how often airships were handled on the ground in gusty winds, on small mats, with tricky hangar spill overs, by tired men who had to keep their footing in water, in mud, or on ice, it is remarkable that there were not more accidents involving members of the ground crews. There were the everpresent dangers of spinning propellers and dangling handling lines to watch out for. Knowing this, ground crewmen kept an eye on each other. One night, for example, Aviation Ordnanceman 2nd Class Baldwin of ZP-22, seeing a man caught in a line, rushed over and cut him loose. Just a half-hour later Baldwin noticed another man about to walk into a propeller. He saved him with a flying tackle.

A number of times ground handlers were caught in the lines and pulled along, but there seems to have been no case in which someone was pulled up in the air by them. Crewmen on the car rails were, however. Pilots could see a man caught in a line and take steps to keep the ship on the ground, but the handrails of the car were out of the pilot's view. There were two occasions when a man was pulled

157

aloft while he was clinging to them. In the one case, he could not let go because the ship's trailing-wire antenna (which had negligently not been reeled in) had wound itself about him and effectively tied him to the rail. He had to be brought into the car through the aft doors while the ship was in the air. The second man, who had waited too long to let go, wedged an arm and a foot between the rail and the car and hung on while the blimp circled the field and landed to let him off.

As a safeguard against being carried off by a line, ground crews carried knives. To avoid being struck by a propeller, however, they had to learn that if they fell in front of a moving airship they should stay down and let the prop pass over them. This was a good safety rule that was drilled into the crews, but it was, unfortunately, contrary to instinct. If you fell, you wanted to get to your feet and start running as fast as possible to get out of danger. If instinct prevailed, the result could be tragic. When a ground handler in Brazil slipped and fell, the entire ground crew shouted to him to stay down, but he rose to his feet, right in the path of the propeller.

Ground-handling officers, who customarily stood in front of the car while giving directions, could be in jeopardy too. One at South Weymouth, having given the signal to take off, slipped on the ice-covered mat while the *K-38*, a few feet away, was fast bearing down on him. He crawled hurriedly on all fours to one side to get out of the way of the wheel. Then he threw himself flat to allow the propeller to miss him.

Working on the mast, especially if it was dew-covered, also had its dangers. Safety belts were worn. It was a good forty feet from the top of the mast to the ground.

There were close shaves with masts just as there were with handling lines, props, and car rails. At Yarmouth, Nova Scotia, the *K-9* was blown across the field while landing. (The pilot was keeping the ship on the ground to help a handler who had been caught up by a line.) The airship went broadside right into the mast. The bag was punctured, and the blimp began to deflate. One of the two men on the mast immediately unbuckled himself to get down. He fell, bouncing off the mast's structure and dropping to the ground. The other disappeared. He had fallen through the hole in the envelope and was inside the bag. When cut out, he was close to suffocating from breathing helium.

One airshipman, a respected leading chief named Calhoun, did die of helium suffocation. At the Mandinga detachment of ZP-23 in Panama, he went inside an airship's gas chamber to check for leaks. The mask he was wearing to supply him with air failed, and he was pulled out lifeless.

Such were the wartime fatalities of the Atlantic Fleet's blimps:

Thirty-five dead in seven airships.

Another estimated three to five killed in accidents on the ground.

To this toll must be added those who died on 27 November 1944 when the PBY-5 Catalina of Fleet Airship Wing Four crashed near São Luiz, Brazil. Twenty-two were killed, including the plane's crew, thirteen officers and men of Blimp Headquarters Squadron Four, and presumably several members of Blimp Squadron Forty-One (the remainder of the passengers).

12. FINALE

THE FINAL MONTHS of the war against Germany began with a bizarre episode at Port Lyautey. On 15 January 1945 an individual posing as a French officer succeeded in deflating the *K-123* with a jeep.

The airship had been rigged in anticipation of high winds. One precaution taken at such times was to attach a cable from the car to the mast so that if the blimp tore loose it would not blow away. Another was to add an extension line to the rip cords so that in an emergency they could be pulled from the ground instead of having to be pulled from inside the car. On the *K-123* an "extender" had been tied to the forward rip cord, fastened by a light line (which could easily be broken) to the forward handrail, and then led along one of the forward handling lines for about forty feet. This way the "extender" and rip cord were within easy reach of ground personnel.

The impostor, who knew nothing about the special rigging proceeded to drive his jeep at a good clip right between the front of the car and the mast, ignoring the shouts of the pressure watch to stop. His windshield caught the extender. Oblivious to what was happening, he drove on, pulling open the rip panel at the top of the bag and leaving a fast-emptying airship dropping to the ground behind him.

K-ships that were deflated by ripping, settling into trees, and striking hangar doors, unless there had been an accompanying fire, could be repaired and put back into the air again once their envelopes had been replaced. But to erect an airship required a hangar. The *K-123* could be erected again because ZP-14 had the hangar at Cuers.

A new bag was ordered from the States, plus the ground cloth, net, and other required paraphernalia. Goodyear sent over two tech-

This fine mess resulted when the *K-123*'s rip-cord extender was snagged by the windshield of a jeep driven by an impostor in a French uniform on 15 January 1945. (U.S. Navy)

nicians to assist. But owing to delays in getting the materials to Cuers, the ship would not fly again until after the war ended.

Perhaps the most difficult part of restoring the *K-123* to flying condition was transporting its fourteen-foot-high, forty-two-foot-long car from Port Lyautey to Cuers. It was trucked from Lyautey to Casablanca, sent by ship from Casablanca to Marseilles, and then trucked again from Marseilles to Cuers. Completing the sixty-mile trip over the narrow roads of southern France proved formidable. Overhead wires had to be relocated, trees trimmed, and the way cleared for the flatbed carrying the car, which traveled under a black shroud. Its movement through the villages and countryside was like a religious procession.

On 26 March ZP-14 lost another airship, this time because of fire. A sudden violent updraft seized the *K-109* as it rode to its mast at Lyautey. Up went the ship's stern as it began to "kite." The two enlisted men standing pressure watch on board were amazed, as the blimp stood on its nose, to see the mast being lifted off the ground. Then the ship crashed back down, tipping over the mast and breaking the outriggers of the starboard engine. The *K-109* bounced, the men on board desperately valving helium to try to keep it down. Sensing that fire was about to break out, they jumped to the ground. The airship hit again, this time knocking an engine off and bursting into

161

When a violent updraft caught the *K-109* on 26 March 1945 and tore it from its mast, this was the result (upper and lower left). The *K-130* was dragged 225 yards, its tracks showing that its mast wheels had been lifted off the ground (right). (U.S. Navy)

flames. It was consumed in two minutes. Another ship, the *K-130*, was moored nearby. It did not blow away but was dragged 225 yards on its mast, cracking the radar hat and bending the propellers. The three on board, an officer and two enlisted men, hurriedly abandoned it when they saw what was happening to the *K-109*. The wind was a freak. Station Aerology, located only a mile away, was recording a maximum of thirty-five knots at the time.

Because the accidents to the *K-123* and *K-109* left ZP-14 short of airships, two more ferry flights were made from the States to Port Lyautey. The *K-89* and *K-114* arrived on 1 May. Their route was different from the path that airships had previously taken across the ocean. After overhaul and preparation at Lakehurst, they were flown to Weeksville, whence they began their Atlantic crossing: Weeksville to Bermuda, Bermuda to Lagens, Lagens to Port Lyautey. This time the midocean leg would be the longest flight ever by a nonrigid airship. Weather, of course, was paramount. John Dungan, Fleet Airships, Atlantic's aerology officer, was back on the job, his detailed forecast later adjudged 95 percent correct. Lt. Comdr. Norman V. Scurria, Fleet Airships, Atlantic's operations officer, was task unit commander for the operation.

The flight from Weeksville to Kindley Field, Bermuda, began on 28 April and took nine hours. After eight hours on stick masts, spent being refueled and checked and, in the case of the *K-114*, having a tachometer replaced, they were off on the long leg, completing the nearly 1,900 miles in 29 hours and 38 minutes on the thirtieth.

The *K-114* and *K-89*, replacing the deflated *K-123* and the burned *K-109*, arrive at Lyautey on 1 May 1945 after refueling stops at Kindley Field, Bermuda, and Lagens, Azores. (U.S. Navy)

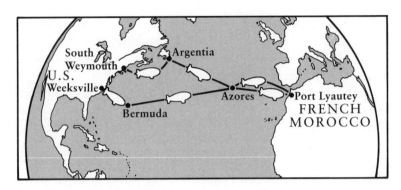

ZP-14's Transatlantic Flight Routes. (U.S. Navy)

First Flight-Southern Route	First Flight-Northern Route
62 hours .... flight time	58 hours .... flight time
77 hours .... elapsed time	80 hours .... elapsed time
28 April–1 May 1945 ..... 3532 miles	29 May–1 June 1944 ...... 3145 miles

While on that leg the airships received a startling message that reported the presence of the German cruiser *Prinz Eugen* in the area. The *K-89* was the lead ship, its pilot, Lt. Wortley W. Townsend, Jr., the flight commander for that portion of the route across. It guarded the control frequency, the interairship frequency, and the distress frequency. The *K-114*, with Lt. James D. Quale as pilot, guarded the interairship and weather frequencies and took radio bearings.

Lt. Ben B. Levitt, one of the Annapolis-trained navigators reserved for these transatlantic ferry operations, checked the enemy's reported position against their flight path. If the information received was correct, the Nazi heavy cruiser was dead ahead. Radar was beginning to show a large target in that direction.

What to do?

Both airships had been stripped of nonessentials for the trip. The closest thing they had to a piece of ordnance was a Very pistol for signaling. The *Prinz Eugen* not only had the firepower of a major warship, she had an aircraft, an Arado 196. Townsend and Quale conferred by radio to decide upon a course of action. They really had no choice. They were more than halfway along, had passed their point of no return in terms of their fuel consumption, and had to keep going. They would steer around the target ahead, thankful for a fog bank that overhung the water and reached to 1,200 feet.

There was, in fact, no *Prinz Eugen* along the blimps' route. She was in the Baltic with most of her ammunition expended, giving gunfire support to retreating German forces. Where did the misinformation come from? Had it been a hoax perpetrated by the squadron "to keep those guys awake out there"? And how to explain the radar return? These questions were never answered.

The arrival of the *K-89* and *K-114* at Port Lyautey took place on 1 May 1945, just three days before Dönitz struck his colors and ordered his submarines to cease hostilities. Although on the ropes, he and his captains had continued to fight to the end, putting their reliance on the Schnorkel and their hopes on the new "electro-boats."

It was at this time that one of the Cuers-based airships, while being ferried from North Africa, unknowingly transported a stow-away, a young Arab boy who, thinking that the blimp was headed for America where he had family, had hidden inside the wheel well. When the ship was landed and masted at Cuers, an astounded ground crew saw two skinny brown legs suddenly drop down onto the ground. The lad, unhurt, was tired and frightened by the ordeal. The flight on which he had stowed away had been one of the roughest crossings of the Mediterranean in ZP-14's experience.

The Schnorkel, known variously as the Schnorchel, the Snorkel, and the Snort, was a Dutch invention, an air pipe that could be raised so its head extended above the surface while the submarine moved along submerged. The device admitted air and conducted it via a tube into the hull, where the diesels used it for combustion. A second tube exhausted the combustion products. In this way U-boats could run their diesels for propulsion and for charging their batteries. Before, they had been forced to surface to charge the batteries, their source of propulsion while submerged. And it was while surfaced that they had proven so vulnerable to British and American radars and weapons.

The "electro-boats" were 1600-tonners (surfaced), known as Type XXIs. They were called "electro-boats" because of the large battery complex that they recharged with their diesels while schnorkeling. For their day, their underwater performance was amazing. They could do 17 knots submerged and at 6 knots could cover 285 miles, a performance made possible by a superbly streamlined hull and efficient propulsion system. The top speed on the surface was about fifteen knots; the range at twelve knots was eleven thousand miles. They were to have fifty-seven officers and men in the crew and to carry twenty-three torpedoes. The great and last hope of the U-boat fleet, only one of their number succeeded in reaching "the front" before Germany's surrender. This was the *U-2511*, under Comdr. Adalbert Schnee, which left its concrete pen in Norway for the Atlantic about 30 April. When he received Dönitz's general order of 4 May to end the fighting, Schnee returned to base. On his way home he made a dummy run on a British cruiser, "torpedoed" it, and escaped without being detected.

The Schnorkel had its pros and cons. To be sure, it enabled a submarine to stay submerged—one did for sixty-six days—without exposing conning tower or hull to enemy radar. On the other hand, it meant misery for the crew. If the Schnorkel head went underwater in rough seas and the float valve controlling the air intake closed, the diesels, deprived of the outside air, sucked up what was inside. The consequent drop in inboard pressure made eyeballs practically jump out of their sockets and eardrums burst. On the other hand if the exhaust tube was closed off, the spaces inside would become contaminated with exhaust fumes. Crews, furthermore, had no chance to go on deck, saw no daylight, and had to do everything underwater and in the blind. Critical to its survival was the U-boat's ability to "listen," but while running underwater on its diesels, the engine noise clobbered the hydrophones.

Norwegian-based Schnorkel-equipped boats were enjoying some success, particularly in the Southwest Approaches to England. To help counter them there, Blimp Squadron Forty-Two, in April 1945, was ordered transferred from Brazil to the United Kingdom. The reason was that the Schnorkel head, although covered with a material intended to absorb radar impulses, could still be detected by radar, particularly that of a slow-moving blimp. The airship was also considered an excellent platform from which to detect visually the feather made by Schnorkels moving through the water and the diesel smoke they emitted.

ZP-42, commanded by Lt. Comdr. Harold B. Van Gorder, was to operate from Chivenor in Devon under Fleet Air Wing Seven with the British Coastal Command. The squadron's executive officer, Lt. Comdr. Larry P. Mack, and other officers went to England as an advance party to prepare for the arrival of the *K-93, K-100, K-126,* and *K-127,* which were being prepared at Lakehurst for the assignment. In England they met with Lt. Comdr. Orville W. Mellick, who had been assigned as LTA staff member to Commander Fleet Air Wing Seven, and Commander Sullivan, on temporary duty from Fleet Air Wing Fifteen to lend his experience in bringing the "Africa Squadron" across the Atlantic the year before. Former British airshipmen Lord Ventry and Ralph S. Booth were consulted and arrangements made to use Cardington, near Bedford, and its old rigid airship hangars as an overhaul base. The transatlantic route was to be Weeksville to Bermuda to the Azores to England. The first two airships were, in fact, on their way over when the war ended and the movement of the squadron was canceled.

Navy blimps were thus denied a go at the enemy in the Southwest Approaches. They participated, however, in the last U-boat "kill" in American waters. This was the *U-853*, one of a handful of boats dispatched from Norway to operate independently in the westernmost Atlantic.

On 5 May this Schnorkel-carrying Type IXC, Oberleutnant Helmut Frömsdorfer commanding, torpedoed and sank the collier *Black Point* near Block Island, south of Newport, Rhode Island. The destroyer *Ericsson*, the destroyer escorts *Atherton* and *Amick*, and the Coast Guard frigate *Moberly* converged on the scene, making sound contact and attacking the U-boat. ZP-12's *K-16*, piloted by Lt. (jg) John T. Clark, and *K-58*, piloted by Lt. (jg) Max I. Zabst, were dispatched from Lakehurst early the next day, the sixth. Upon the blimps' arrival, the *Ericsson* asked the *K-16*, to make an MAD search of the target area. Strong MAD signals were received on a large metallic object that was stationary. Attacks by the surface ships followed. More MAD runs showed the object still there and still stationary. The *Ericsson* followed up with another depth charging that brought up oil and air bubbles.

The *K-16*, at this point, dropped a sonobuoy. Intermittent metallic hammering could be heard, also a loud squeal, before the screws of the vessels on hand drowned out the sounds. From 150 feet the *K-16* attacked the source of the oil and air, dropping four depth bombs with M-140 contact fuzes at twenty-foot spacings. All four detonated three seconds after entering the water.

The *K-58* then moved in. It registered five MAD contacts, which it marked with dye and floats. It also attacked with two bombs of the same type that the *K-16* had dropped, one of which detonated three seconds after penetrating the surface.

The enemy vanquished: the *U-858*, flying the Stars and Stripes after surrendering to U.S. naval forces at the war's end, proceeds under airship escort to Lewes, Delaware. (U.S. Navy)

Another round of depth charging by the surface ships followed the *K-16*'s and *K-58*'s attacks. The water became littered with debris that included an officer's cap, a piece of table, a mattress, life jackets, escape lungs, a pulley, and a wooden flag pole painted gray. The *U-853* had been destroyed in the last U-boat action involving American naval forces.

With hostilities ended and no more antisubmarine missions to be performed, ZP-14's two new arrivals were put to work assisting the other airships in mine-clearing operations. Between November 1944 and February 1945 the squadron had been flying these missions from Cuers, France; Bizerte, Tunisia; and Cagliari, Sardinia. In March it had moved to Rome's Littorio Field, from which the *K-101* located a sunken American minesweeper off Anzio with MAD. To enable the wreck to be salvaged, the blimp also plotted a mine-free channel to it. ZP-14's operations at Cagliari were completed in early April 1945.

On 4 May, responding to a British request for help in clearing the waters in the Genoa region, the *K-101* proceeded to Pisa, fifty miles from Genoa. The U.S. Army was already there in full force, the field populated by B-17 bombers and Thunderbolt fighters. The airship found itself a home in a hay field adjoining the main landing strip, its mast anchored by concrete pillars retrieved from bombed-out buildings. At Pisa the *K-101* was dubbed "Minnie the Miner," a name immortalized by artwork executed on the side of the car by an army sergeant. The mine field plots made from the airship were checked with those left behind by the Germans. They tallied closely. Meanwhile, mine-spotting flights continued to be made from Cuers for the American and French navies.

Demobilization of Fleet Airships, Atlantic began quickly. Actually, it had commenced the year before as the U-boat threat had

To help clear Genoa's waters, the *K-101* operated out of the army-occupied airfield at Pisa, Italy. (U.S. Navy)

Top left, a liaison officer gives instructions to minesweeping craft below. (U.S. Navy) Top right, the *K-101* acquired this name and artwork at Pisa. (U.S. Navy) Bottom, as Fifth Army G.I.s look on, the *K-110* flies over the you-know-what. (U.S. Navy)

diminished. Three blimp squadrons had been decommisioned in 1944: ZP-22 in September and ZP-51 and ZP-23 in December. Other squadrons had assumed their missions.

By the end of January 1946, all Atlantic Fleet blimp squadrons had been decommisioned except for ZP-12 at Lakehurst. ZP-14 had closed down on 22 January but not before operating temporarily from Venice and Malta. ZP-41 was the last to go. It hung on while a forty-man Brazilian air force team completed training at Lakehurst in anticipation that it would take over and operate the squadron's airships and equipment.* When Brazil reneged on the deal, ZP-41 was decommissioned on 31 January.

---

* While training Brazilians at Lakehurst, Lt. Harris F. Smith, took a special interest in free balloons. He acquired such proficiency and reputation with them that in late 1946, after his release to inactive duty, he would be recalled to pilot an Office of Naval Research stratosphere balloon to one hundred thousand feet. This pioneering flight, named Helios, while later canceled for technical reasons, led the navy to its most important LTA development of the immediate postwar period: high-altitude research using very large, plastic, unmanned balloons that it called Skyhooks.

EPILOGUE

⟆ From 2 January 1942 to 15 May 1945 Atlantic Fleet airships made 37,554 flights, flew 378,237 hours, and escorted more than 70,000 vessels.

I have made no attempt to evaluate that record. Readers interested in doing so might begin with what Admiral Dönitz wrote me in 1964:

> Each air patrol was disturbing to the operation of U-boats because they were forced underwater, making it no longer possible for them to reach their attack positions. As a consequence, the American "blimps" were very disturbing to German U-boat activity. Naturally airplanes, compared with "blimps," had the advantage of higher speed. Thus they represented for U-boats a greater danger than "blimps."
>
> It is possible that a U-boat commander, at the sight of a "blimp" might conclude that a convoy was nearby. On the other hand, there was also the possibility that the sighted "blimp" was only on patrol. But even if the commander, upon seeing the "blimp," surmised a convoy, that would only be a slight disadvantage to the use of a "blimp" since it would hinder the U-boat's approach, at the very least severely.

In evaluating a weapon system's performance, the opinion of the enemy is a good place to start.

A. PACIFIC OPERATIONS

~~~~~~ As There Was a Commander Fleet Airships, Atlantic
so there was a Commander Fleet Airships, Pacific, successively Captains Thomas G. W. Settle, Scott E. Peck, and Howard N. Coulter,
headquartered at Naval Air Station Moffett Field, California. Reporting to them were Fleet Airship Wing Three, Blimp Headquarters
Squadron Three, and Blimp Squadrons Thirty-One, Thirty-Two,
and Thirty-Three. The wing (which was one and the same with
Fleet Airships, Pacific), the headquarters squadron, and ZP-32 were
based at Moffett; ZP-31 and ZP-33 were based, respectively, at NAS
Santa Ana, California, and NAS Tillamook, Oregon.*

The naval air stations at Santa Ana and Tillamook had been built
from scratch, products of prewar planning, chiefly Rosendahl's. Each
was the possessor of two standard one-thousand-foot-long hangars.
Moffett Field had two of these wood-and-concrete creations in addition to the large steel hangar that had once housed the *Macon*. After
that airship was lost in 1935, the navy transferred the base to the
army, which called it Sunnyvale. With the navy again needing an
airship base in the San Francisco area, the army returned it, albeit
somewhat reluctantly.

There were no navy airships on the Pacific Coast at the time of
Pearl Harbor. The entire seaboard was virtually naked of defense
against whatever mischief the Japanese might have had in mind.
Rosendahl, always the man of action, lost no time in having the *TC-
13* and *TC-14* sent west from Lakehurst to establish a squadron
at Sunnyvale (Moffett Field). Deflated and disassembled, the two

---

* Auxiliary bases existed at Del Mar, Lompoc, Watsonville, and Eureka in California; North Bend and Astoria in Oregon; and Shelton and Quillayute in Washington. At Del Mar there was also an antisubmarine training activity, the Fleet
Airships Pacific Tactical Unit.

airships made the cross-country trip in eleven railroad cars. Lt. Comdr. George F. Watson, the squadron's prospective commanding officer, also proceeded to California from Lakehurst with about seven officers and twenty enlisted men, all LTA qualified.

Watson, whom the reader has met in connection with his survey of bases in Brazil and his staffing of the movement of ZP-14 to North Africa while a member of the Tenth Fleet, arrived in California and reported to the Commander Western Sea Frontier, who, in turn, had him report to Commander Fleet Air Wing Two, Capt. John Dale Price. Airship Patrol Squadron Thirty-Two was commissioned to the playing of "Anchors Aweigh" by an army band at Sunnyvale on 31 January 1942. The *TC-14*, which made its first flight there on 2 February, was joined in the air a week later by the *TC-13*. Sunnyvale was officially transferred back to the navy on 16 April.

Watson later remembered those early days in this way:

> We started flying regular daylight patrol over the sea lanes entering San Francisco harbor. The Western Sea Frontier seemed happy to have us provide a kind of surveillance which they had not had.

The ex-army *TC-14*, shown here in navy markings at Lakehurst, began airship operations on the Pacific Coast. It was secured to its mast by a belly mooring arrangement instead of the conventional nose cone. (U.S. Navy)

Among other things, we could fly under the 500-foot ceiling that persisted in the area. We had interesting times coming back through the Coastal Range and getting down at Moffett. We hit the mountains once but bounced off. One night the TC-13 came down right in the middle of the barrage balloons over the naval shipyard at Mare Island. The guys on the ground did not open fire but they called us and told us to get our blimp out of there which the pilot promptly did.

The Navy, in the meanwhile, had bought the Goodyear airship fleet. We got the Los Angeles- and Miami-based ships and a new "L." Goodyear pilots who were not already in the Naval Reserve, enrolled and were commissioned. Many of the Goodyear crewmen enlisted. The Goodyear ships came with masts, rolling stock, and field equipment, so we were quickly able to patrol the coastal lanes from the Oregon border to the Mexican. We established naval air facilities with masts along the coast. The one at Del Mar was at the race track which was then owned by Bing Crosby. He rented the field to us for $1 a year and fixed up the jockey quarters very elegantly for our people. Del Mar was a popular assignment.

In the first months of West Coast operations, an L-ship frequently operated from a mast at San Francisco's Treasure Island. It flew what was popularly known as "the sardine patrol," accompanying the fishing boats as they left the bay area each morning, returning to base, and then going out again to meet them coming back in. L-ships, smallest of the navy's blimps, did not have the endurance to stay out all day.

The most famous of these small airships was the *L-8*. Lt. Comdr. John B. Rieker flew a special mission with it in April. His orders: to rendezvous with the carrier *Hornet* and deliver a package. Expecting to find plenty of room on the flight deck for his three hundred–pound drop, Rieker found it, instead, jammed with airplanes, *army* airplanes. What he had done was deliver spare parts for aircraft that would make the Doolittle raid on Tokyo.

The *L-8* was best known, however, for having gone on patrol and returned with no one on board. At 0600 on 16 August 1942 it took off from Treasure Island with Lt. Ernest D. Cody and Ens. Charles E. Adams as crew.

At 0750 the airship reported by radio that it was investigating an oil slick five miles east of the Farallon Islands, an area where oil slicks were common.

175

At 0805 an unsuccessful attempt was made to contact the *L-8*, the first of many.

At 1020 a Pan American Airways plane sighted the airship, and at 1030 a navy plane, one of two sent out to look for it, saw it break through the overcast, then descend into it again.

At about 1045 a telephone call from Fort Funston, on the western shore of the San Francisco Peninsula, advised that an airship had landed and taken off again. A half-hour later another call, this one from Daly City, reported that the *L-8*, empty, was lying in one of its streets.

The navy team that went to the scene found the *L-8* deflated; its car door open; one of its two bombs missing; both engines stopped, with one throttle open and the other half open; ignition switches "on"; gasoline in the tanks and the valves from the tanks to the

The *L-8*, deformed owing to lack of pressure, drifts empty and eastward from patrol. (U.S. Navy)

engines open; the radio operative; the life raft on board; and the folder of confidential material intact. There were holes in the envelope where the Daly City Fire Department had slashed it open to see if anyone was inside.

From Fort Funston came the additional information that the L-8, drifting in from the Pacific and descending slowly, had come down on the beach, where two bathers had tried to take hold of its handling lines. They noticed that the engines were dead, that there was nobody on board, and that the car door was open. When the airship struck the beach, one of its bombs fell off. Lightened, the ship rose and continued its silent drift eastward, its envelope bent into a V-shape because of the lack of pressure inside.

There had been a navy ship, a Coast Guard boat, and various fishing vessels in the area where the L-8 had been checking the oil slick. They had seen it come down low, drop two smoke flares, and then climb and fly off into the overcast. When one of the navy search planes saw the L-8 emerge from the cloud tops, the airship's altitude would have had to have been two thousand feet. A lot of importance was given to this observation. The "pressure height" of the L-8 that morning was probably about one thousand feet. At that altitude the air ballonets would have been full. To go higher would have meant valving off helium to keep the gas pressure within bounds. If Cody and Adams had been in control of their ship at that time, it was unlikely that they would have taken it to that altitude.

No Japanese submarines were in the area. None of the surface craft had seen anything suspicious.

That Cody and Adams had abandoned ship on purpose did not seem possible. They would have taken along the life raft, destroyed the confidential folder, and radioed a call for help. Knowing that the wind would drift them back to the mainland, barring something very unusual, they would have stayed with the blimp.

The most accepted explanation was that one of them had gone to the door and opened it. Losing his balance, he began to fall out. The other, rushing to his aid, went through the door with him. Although they were wearing life vests, their bodies were never recovered.

K-ships began arriving on the West Coast in October. Only three, the K-20, K-21, and K-22, were flown in from Akron. Lt. Comdr. Emmett J. Sullivan was in charge of the ferry operation and

177

The wreckage of the *L-8* in the street at Daly City, California. (U.S. Navy)

responsible for getting them safely over and through the mountains.* Subsequent "Ks" were shipped from Goodyear to Moffett Field and assembled there. As the K-ships arrived, the "TCs" and "Ls" were phased out for operational patrols.

Airship Patrol Squadron Thirty-One was commissioned at Santa Ana on 1 October 1942, Airship Patrol Squadron Thirty-Three at Tillamook on 1 November. As the three squadrons—later they would be called blimp squadrons and designated ZP-31, ZP-32, and ZP-33—built up to full complement in pilots, crews, and K-ships,

* Sullivan, the prospective commanding officer of Squadron Thirty-Three, quickly proved to be one of the outstanding officers serving in LTA. Recognition came in 1944 when he was given command of ZP-14 and told to take it to North Africa.

flying time on the West Coast mounted: 6,763 hours in 1942, 43,991 in 1943, and 69,089 in 1944.

Despite all this flight time, no airship could claim a contact with an enemy submarine. Except for the first days of hostilities when the Japanese submarine *I-17* lobbed seventeen shells from offshore into oil storage tanks near Santa Barbara (24 February 1942) and reportedly also sank a couple of merchant ships farther up the coast, there were few, if any, of the enemy in airship-patrolled waters.

A navy blimp did, however, carry out a verified attack against an American submarine. This was the venerable ex-army *TC-14*, piloted by the ubiquitous Johnny Rieker. Seeing a periscope a short distance outside the entrance to San Francisco Bay and knowing that no friendly submarine was supposed to be operating independently and submerged in waters that close to shipping lanes, he went after it. His bombs exploded but did no damage. A very surprised U.S. Navy

Three blimps and five free balloons being inflated in NAS Moffett Field's steel hangar, which once housed the *Macon*. Moffett was a key assembly and repair activity during the war. Note the airship fins hanging on the wall and stacked by the doors. (U.S. Navy)

submarine surfaced in great dander. The submariners, of course, wanted Rieker's hide, but Rieker had a champion, John Dale Price, the commander of Fleet Air Wing Two, who defused the incident. Price stoutly defended Rieker's actions, stating that he had done the right thing under the circumstances.

The West Coast was teeming with every imaginable kind of military activity. With so much going on, accidents were numerous, and there were people to be saved. During 1943 the blimps of Fleet Airships, Pacific came to the rescue more than a dozen times, and during 1944 about thirty times.

When a plane faltered and fell into the sea while taking off from a carrier, for example, an airship from ZP-31 was overhead of it within two to three minutes and dropped a life raft to the pilot. This achievement by Lt. (jg) P. I. Culbertson was billed "The Fastest Air/ Sea Rescue in LTA."

Another of ZP-31's crews, commanded by Ens. Lowell E. Buys in the *K-59*, performed the first sea-to-airship rescue. Finding two men, one injured and bleeding profusely, in a raft off Oceanside, California, Buys approached to within twenty-five feet and lowered a parachute harness. The bleeding man was pulled up and brought aboard.

On 12 May 1944 Ens. John Hoag, also of ZP-31, went to the help of a PBY Catalina trying to rescue an F6F fighter pilot who had crash-landed thirty-five miles off San Clemente Island. Seeing that the flying boat was shipping water and was unable to maneuver in the rough sea, Hoag, from twenty feet up, dropped a raft to the pilot. It inflated automatically, but the man in the water was in no condition to use it. To try to help him, Aviation Radioman 1st Class J. A. Sosnoski jumped from the starboard door into the water from a height of about ten feet, a swell taking the raft out of his reach as he hit the surface. With Sosnoski clinging to the starboard short line, Hoag towed him through the water over to the PBY, which, by this time, had reached the victim and found him dead. The plane took Sosnoski aboard. It had, however, taken on so much water that it had to be abandoned and sunk by gunfire. A destroyer picked up Sosnoski and the Catalina's crew.

On the following day the *K-95* (of ZP-31) used a parachute harness to pull up marine Capt. Frank B. Baldwin, an ace in the war against Japan, after he had ditched his fighter.

Not all rescues were at sea. On 2 July 1944 the *K-95* and pilot Culbertson landed near Holtville, California, to evacuate three survivors of a navy plane crash from the desert.

To ZP-31 went the credit, also, for making the first landing of a U.S. Navy blimp on an aircraft carrier, the USS *Altamaha*, on 4 February 1944. This landing demonstrated a capability that would be important operationally in postwar years.

Airship operations on the West Coast regretfully had their share of accidents and deaths. The disappearance of the two officers aboard the *L-8* has been cited. When the *K-111* collided in poor visibility with a hillside on Santa Catalina Island, six men died. And at Santa Ana the *K-51*, after dumping gas preparatory to landing, caught

The landing by ZP-31's *K-29* aboard the USS *Altamaha* off San Diego on 4 February 1944 was the first ever by a U.S. Navy blimp on a carrier. (U.S. Navy)

fire, killing eight crew members. There were probably also ground-handling fatalities.

On 6 October, the war in the Pacific having ended, the Commander-in-Chief, U.S. Fleet directed the decommissioning of Fleet Airships, Pacific; Fleet Airship Wing Three; Blimp Headquarters Squadron Three; and Blimp Squadrons Thirty-Two and Thirty-Three. Only Blimp Squadron Thirty-One remained. U.S. Navy airship operations along the West Coast had totaled (31 January 1942 to 1 September 1945) 20,156 flights, 167,291 hours, and about 11,000 vessels escorted.

B. DESTRUCTION OF NAS RICHMOND

～～ ALTHOUGH IT HAPPENED after the war and outside the time frame of this book, the fiery end of Naval Air Station Richmond, Florida, on 14 September 1945 must be included.

The thousand-foot-long hangars at LTA stations had proven safe places of refuge during hurricanes. In September 1944, when one boiled its way up the eastern seaboard, 360 navy airplanes were evacuated to the hangars at South Weymouth and 161 to those at NAS Weeksville.

Squeezing that many planes among the blimps already occupying those hangars took some doing. At South Weymouth, officers with flags were positioned on the field to direct the incoming traffic so that the planes would be hangared with others from their own outfits. Folding-wing aircraft, like the Grumman F6F, were to be put in the barn first because they could be more easily spotted around the airships inside. It was a good idea, but one that was soon abandoned in the rush and crush of arriving planes. Traffic lanes were established leading into the hangars. At first planes taxied up to the doors, cut their engines, and were pushed inside. When this proved too slow, they began taxiing in. Winds that night peaked at sixty-one knots, not enough to do serious damage.

At Weeksville, however, where wind speeds reached seventy knots, glass in the wooden hangar began to break loose from the skylights and fall on an L-ship directly below. The glass continued to rain down, puncturing the airship's bag faster than it could be patched. Timber also fell to the deck. Because of the hazardous situation, the men were ordered to stop working on the blimp and to leave the hangar. When they returned after the winds had subsided, they found the "L" deflated and twenty-eight navy airplanes damaged by falling debris. Glass had also fallen inside the station's

183

steel hangar, but moving the airships about had kept them clear of the major danger areas.

The damage at Weeksville was a taste of things to come.

Exactly one year later the three hangars at Richmond were packed with aircraft seeking protection from a hurricane. Winds that reached 140 knots, perhaps even higher, beat the structures to pieces. The roofs collapsed; the beams and debris fell inside, rupturing fuel tanks and shorting electrical circuits. Fires broke out. Thirty-eight naval personnel were injured while fighting the flames. One man, Harry H. Schultz, the civilian station fire chief, was killed.

Smashed and burned were 25 blimps, some in storage; 31 non-navy U.S. Government airplanes; 125 privately owned planes; and 212 navy HTA craft.

C. BLIMP OPERATING AREAS

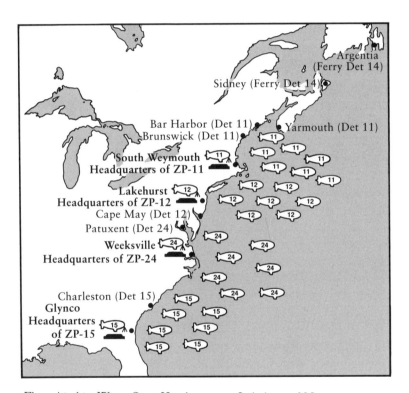

Fleet Airship Wing One. Headquarters, Lakehurst, N.J.

Squadrons		Main Operating Base
ZP-11	8 airships	Naval Air Station, South Weymouth, Massachusetts
ZP-12	8 airships	Naval Air Station, Lakehurst, New Jersey
ZP-24	8 airships	Naval Air Station, Weeksville, North Carolina
ZP-15	8 airships	Naval Air Station, Glyco, Georgia

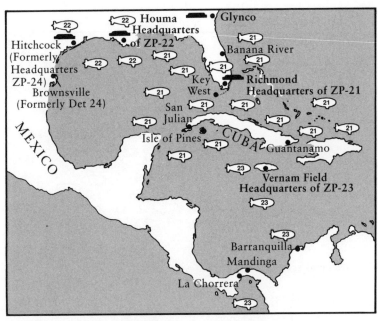

Fleet Airship Wing Two. Headquarters, Richmond, Fla.

Squadrons		*Main Operating Base*
ZP-21	15 airships	Richmond, Florida
ZP-22	4 airships	Houma, Louisiana
ZP-23	4 airships	Vernam Field, Jamaica, B.W.I.

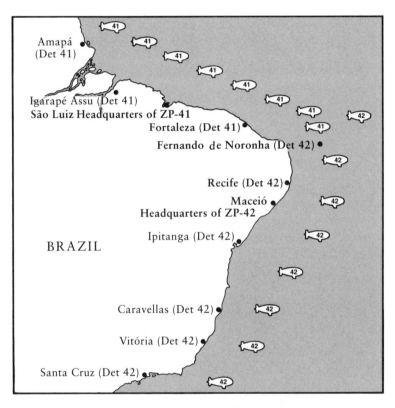

Fleet Airship Wing Four. Headquarters, Recife, Brazil.

Squadrons		*Main Operating Base*
ZP-41	8 airships	São Luiz, Brazil
ZP-42	8 airships	Maceió, Brazil

187

Fleet Airship Wing Five. Headquarters, Trinidad, B.W.I.

Squadrons	Main Operating Base
ZP-51 .... 8 airships	Trinidad, B.W.I.

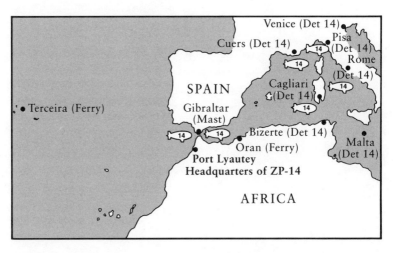

Squadron 14-No. Africa. Headquarters, Port Lyautey, French Morocco

Squadrons	Main Operating Base
ZP-14 .... 6 airships	Port Lyautey, French Morocco

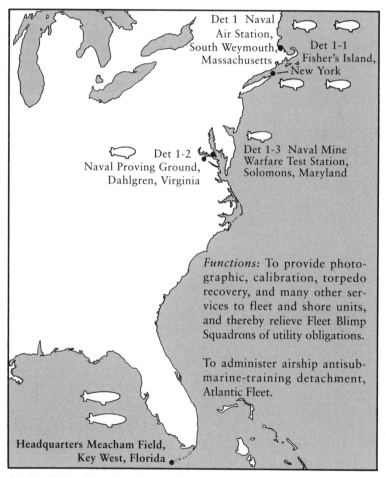

Det 1 Naval Air Station, South Weymouth, Massachusetts

Det 1-1 Fisher's Island, New York

Det 1-2 Naval Proving Ground, Dahlgren, Virginia

Det 1-3 Naval Mine Warfare Test Station, Solomons, Maryland

Functions: To provide photographic, calibration, torpedo recovery, and many other services to fleet and shore units, and thereby relieve Fleet Blimp Squadrons of utility obligations.

To administer airship antisubmarine-training detachment, Atlantic Fleet.

Headquarters Meacham Field, Key West, Florida

Airship Utility Squadron One. 6 G-ships, 2 K-ships, Headquarters, Meacham Field, Key West, Fla.

D. THE K-SHIP

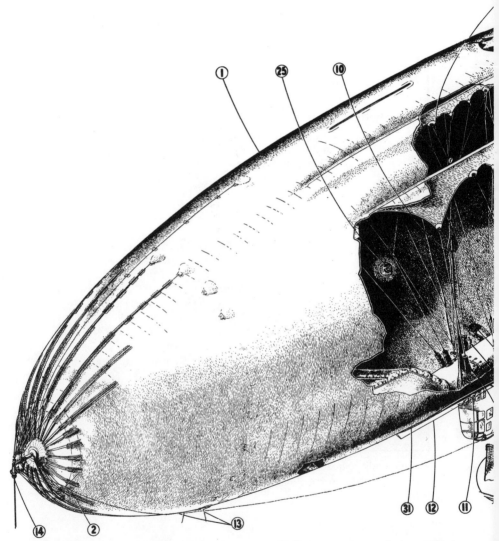

Cutaway drawing of the K Airship. (1) Envelope; (2) Bow mooring and nose stiffening; (3) Empennage; (4) Rip panel; (5) Tail wheel; (6) Car; (7) Landing Gear; (8) Pitot tube; (9) Superheat meter, air element; (10) Superheat meter, gas element; (11) Remote compass; (12) Radio aerial; (13) Handling lines; (14) Mast mooring pendant; (15) Outside car suspension; (16) Car lacing and fairing; (17) Engine nacelle and outrigger; (18) Ballonets, fore and aft—fore partially collapsed; (19) Air lines; (20) 45° internal suspen-

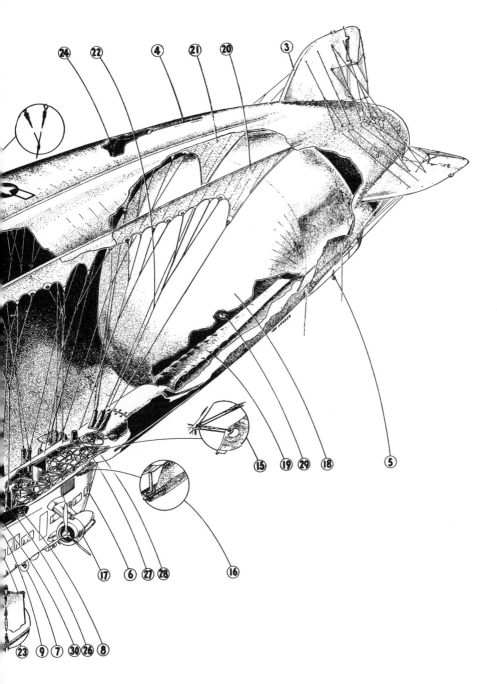

ion catenary; (21) 15° Internal suspension catenary; (22) Internal car suspension catenary;
23) Suspension cable sleeves; (24) Rip cords, fore and aft; (25) Helium discharge valve;
26) Propeller guard frames; (27) Envelope inspection window; (28) Airline manhole;
29) Ballonet manhole; (30) Envelope manhole; (31) Rain drip strip (Original drawing
y Joe Yeager published in *Aero Digest* in 1945)

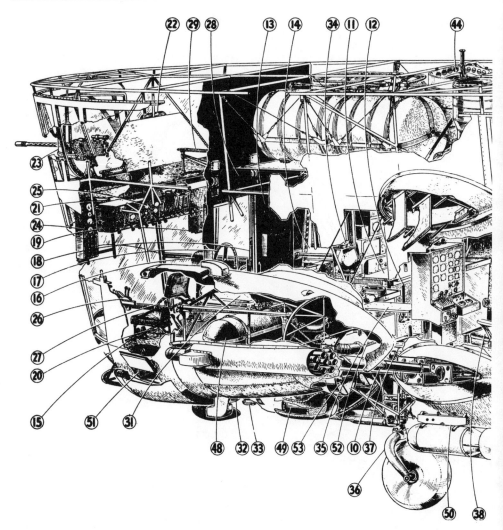

Cutaway drawing of car of the K Airship. (1) Entrance ladder; (2) Aft doors; (3) Drag rope box; (4) Fuel pump duct; (5) Fabric ceiling; (6) Bunks; (7) Auxiliary powerplants; (8) Auxiliary blower; (9) Hot air register; (10) Hot air duct; (11) Radio operator's station; (12) Bomb-bay door control; (13) Sliding door; (14) Emergency door; (15) Bomb releases; (16) Rudder control capstan; (17) Rudder control wheel; (18) Rudder control cables; (19) Rudderman's instrument panel; (20) Bombardier's station; (21) Gunner's ladder; (22) Gunner's station; (23) Machine gun turret; (24) Flight instrument panel; (25) Pilot's instrument panel; (26) Pilot's throttle control; (27) Elevator control wheel, with brake; (28) Elevator control cables; (29) Control cable tensioning device; (30) Control cable

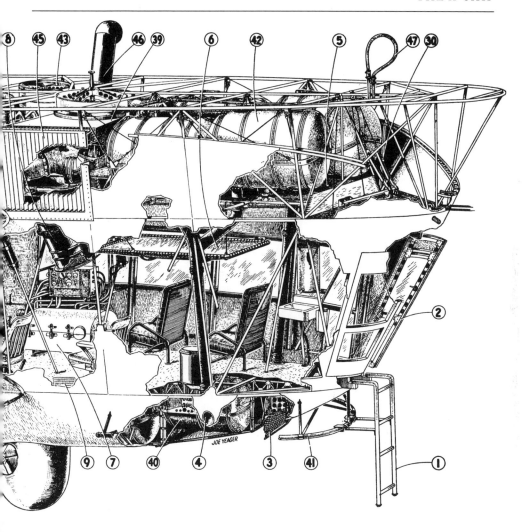

slack take-up; (31) Navigator's station; (32) Landing light; (33) Car running light; (34) Water can; (35) Galley equipment; (36) Landing gear; (37) Battery installation; (38) Mechanic's station; (39) Air discharge elbow; (40) Fuel slip tank; (41) Handling rail; (42) Fuel fixed tanks; (43) Inlet damper, air to ballonet; (44) Air valve, from ballonet; (45) Air discharge louvres; (46) Air to helium inlet, emergency; (47) Trap, fuel tank vents; (48) Oil tank; (49) Oil cooler; (50) External bomb racks; (51) Yaw line box; (52) Engine access platform; (53) Bomb-bay (Original drawing by Joe Yeager published in *Aero Digest* in 1945)

E. WORLD WAR II NAVAL AIRSHIPS

ZNP-K

Volume (cu. ft.)	425,000
Length (ft.)	252
Engines (2)	Pratt and Whitney R-1340-AN-2
Maximum Speed (knots)	67.5
Cruising Range (n. mi.)	1,900 at 50 knots
Number in Service	134 (*K-2* thru *K-135*)
Remarks	Also made in 404,000–, 416,000–, and 456,000–cubic foot sizes

ZNP-M

Volume (cu. ft.)	647,500
Length (ft.)	290
Engines (2)	Pratt and Whitney R-1340-AN-2
Maximum Speed (knots)	69
Cruising Range (n. mi.)	2,000 at 50 knots
Number in Service	4
Remarks	Also made in 625,000– and 725,000–cubic foot sizes

ZNN-G

Volume (cu. ft.)	196,700
Length (ft.)	192
Engines (2)	Continental R-670-6
Maximum Speed (knots)	53
Cruising Range (n. mi.)	680 at 40 knots
Number in Service	7 (*G-2* thru *G-8*)

ZNN-L

Volume (cu. ft.)	123,000
Length (ft.)	149
Engines (2)	Warner R-500-2/6
Maximum Speed (knots)	52
Cruising Range (n. mi.)	520 at 40 knots
Number in Service	22

G-1

Volume (cu. ft.)	183,000
Length (ft.)	186
Engines (2)	Continental
Maximum Speed (knots)	57
Cruising Range (n. mi.)	940 at 48 knots
Remarks	Former Goodyear airship *Defender*

TC-13 and TC-14

Volume (cu. ft.)	357,000
Length (ft.)	235
Engines (2)	Pratt and Whitney
Maximum Speed (knots)	58
Cruising Range (n. mi.)	2,000 at 40 knots
Remarks	Former U.S. Army airships

SOURCES

—— To HELP RECALL the past, I have had the assistance of four good friends—airshipmen all—Capt. James H. Cruse, USN (Ret.); Comdr. Ben B. Levitt, USN (Ret.); Norman J. Mayer, formerly of Goodyear Aircraft and the Bureau of Aeronautics; and Capt. George F. Watson, USN (Ret.). Another close friend, Rick Morris, also formerly of Goodyear, has provided me with valuable information about his company and its production of airships for the navy during the war years. To weaponry expert C. G. Sweeting I acknowledge my gratitude for the details he supplied about the ordnance that airships carried. In addition, I want to note my liberal use of Richard C. Kline's official "Blimpron 14 Overseas" in writing and illustrating chapter 9.

Fleet Airships, Atlantic's "Report on Airship Rescue Operations" (September 1945) and the Naval Airship Training and Experimental Command's "Statistical Summary of United States Fleet Airship Operations in World War II" (February 1946) have been particularly useful. Copies are in the Lighter-than-Air Collection of the Operational Archives Branch, Naval Historical Center, Washington Navy Yard, Washington, D.C., together with the blimp squadrons war diaries and histories. Unfortunately, wartime documentation too often cites only the initials and not the given names of personnel, particularly enlisted, a handicap under which I have had to labor in recounting events.

I have intentionally limited my discussion of Germany's U-boat campaign to the ways and times in which it impacted upon or was impacted by blimp operations. The overall Battle of the Atlantic is a subject so immense and characterized by so many phases, twists, and turns that I have treated it "broad brush" lest its details overwhelm the airship story. For background reading about the

197

U-boat war, the following recent publications are specially recommended:

Doenitz, Grand Admiral Karl. *Memoirs: Ten Years and Twenty Days.* Annapolis: Naval Institute Press, 1990. (Noteworthy for the afterword by Jürgen Rohwer regarding the effects of radio intelligence, including the decoding of the German naval Enigma cypher, on the underseas war.)

Gannon, Michael. *Operation Drumbeat.* New York: Harper and Row, 1990. (*Paukenschlag* as recreated around Reinhard Hardegen and the *U-123.*)

Hickam, Homer H., Jr. *Torpedo Junction: U-Boat War off America's East Coast, 1942.* Annapolis: Naval Institute Press, 1989.

Showell, Jack P. Mallman. *U-Boats under the Swastika.* Annapolis: Naval Institute Press, 1988.

van der Wat, Dan. *The Atlantic Campaign: World War II's Great Struggle at Sea.* New York: Harper and Row, 1988.

For further information about navy blimps before, during, and after World War II there is William F. Althoff's *Sky Ships: A History of the Airship in the United States Navy.* New York: Orion Books, 1990.

INDEX

199

ABOUT THE AUTHOR

J. GORDON VAETH, Lt., USNR (Ret.) was Air Intelligence Officer for Airship Patrol Group One, Fleet Airship Wing 30, and Fleet Airships, Atlantic from 1942 to 1945. In 1946, assigned to Naval Air Station Lakehurst, he became its historical officer and established its airship museum.

Vaeth has been a frequent author of articles about lighter-than-air craft. One of his six previously published books, *Graf Zeppelin*, an account of Germany's commercial dirigible operations in the 1920s and 1930s, was cited by the *New York Times* as among the most recommended works of 1958.

Vaeth's career has included developing high-altitude research balloons for the Office of Naval Research, serving as program manager for weapons-systems simulators at the Naval Training Device Center, providing technical staffing on manned space flight to the Defense Department's Advanced Research Projects Agency, and directing systems engineering for the weather-satellite activities of the National Oceanic and Atmospheric Administration. But he considers his wartime duty with airships his most exciting and memorable.

THE NAVAL INSTITUTE PRESS

BLIMPS AND U-BOATS

U.S. Navy Airships in the Battle of the Atlantic

Designed by Pamela L. Schnitter

Set in Fournier
by Maryland Composition
Glen Burnie, Maryland

Printed on 60-lb. S. D. Warren Sebago eggshell cream
and bound in Holliston Kingston natural and Elephant Hide granite
by The Maple-Vail Book Manufacturing Group
York, Pennsylvania